The Worlds of Tarot

by
Shanddaramon

The Worlds of Tarot:
Expanding the Tarot Universe

by Shanddaramon

The Worlds of Tarot
Expanding the Tarot Universe
by Shanddaramon

First Edition
Published by:
Astor Press
http://www.astorpress.com

ASTOR
PRESS

ISBN: 978-0-578-00527-0
Library of Congress Control Number: 2009920469

Produced in the United States of America

For more information about the author,
visit http://www.shanddaramon.com.

Acknowledgments

I wish to thank one of my first teachers, Enosdeval, for introducing me to the Tarot cards and starting me on a journey that continues to open new doors and insights in my life. I also wish to thank the students of my many summer SUUSI (The Southeast Unitarian-Universalist Summer Institute) Tarot classes who encouraged me to write this book. I wish to thank the students of my Pagan Studies Class who helped me test many of the activities and games in this book. Specifically, I wish to thank Erin Stuelke, Rhaevyn Sunrise, Gwenhwyvar, Heather Davis, Mary Beth Samsa, Sister Dragonfly, and Stephen Phillips.

I would like to thank and congratulate Joseph Ernest Martin for creating the Quest Tarot Deck. It is the deck used through out this text because of its flexibility and wealth of information.

I am also indebted to Reverend Gretchen Woods for her guidance in understanding the process of moral decision making which helped me think through some tough choices during the writing of this text.

Dedication

This book is dedicated to all the people who suffer the stares and taunts of those who do not understand how the secrets of the universe can be found in a little pack of cards.

Table of Contents

Chapter 4

Chapter 5

Chapter 9

Appendix 1

Appendix 2

Foreword

Preface

have been a fan, admirer, student, and practitioner of Tarot for over many, many years now. I have always been fascinated with symbolism - how a simple image can contain deep layers of meaning. Of course, we are the ones who instill that meaning into those symbols but it has always amazed me how we can attribute so many things to just a few images. The seemingly innocent deck of 78 (or so) cards known as the Tarot contains a wide variety of symbols and images from which we can derive meanings. What is more fascinating to me, however, is the way in which cards can be joined in different combinations to create even more meanings. Once I started working with these symbols and realized the seemingly endless ways in which they could be used, I became hooked. I took the standard route of most Tarot students: I studied the cards, the spreads, and the reading techniques. I read cards professionally for a year and then decided that I preferred, instead, to just study the cards and do free readings only for friends. It was during that time that I began exploring other ways of using the cards and new worlds began to open for me. I learned how to use the deck for self-exploration, for helping others, and for, well, just playing. (I think we sometimes take those cards a little too seriously.) The Tarot can teach us secrets to the universe while it can also teach us how to relax and have fun. Staying happy is no less challenging and important than remaining focused on an object of meditation. So, I developed new ways to use the cards and have compiled many of them here.

Introduction

When I first began writing this book, I was determined not to write yet another beginning Tarot book that would describe meanings for each card and talk about spread and readings. There are plenty of books like that already but I believe I have found a unique of reading the cards that allow people to understand cards regardless of which deck they may happen to use. This method has worked very well for my Tarot classes and many students who have never used Tarot cards were able to successfully read a complex spread after only a week of training. Of course, all readers improve through years of practice and experience but a solid early foundation in reading Tarot cards can help people feel confident and interested in the cards. I will introduce that system here for those who may be new to the Tarot. Experienced readers should feel free to continue whatever system works best for them.

This book will go well beyond the basics, however. Its primary purpose is to expand the possible uses of the Tarot beyond just doing simple readings for yourself or others. With these many new ways to use the cards, I suggest that you have several decks to use for several purposes. These decks can include: one deck for your own personal readings, a deck or two for reading for others, a meditation and ritual deck, and a deck just for fun and games.

Invariably when writing a book like this, the question about which deck to use will come up. I have used many different decks. For a long time I was attracted to Aleister Crowley's Thoth deck. The deck that seems to be the standard for most is the pack known as the Rider-Waite deck. On a personal side note, I think it is a disservice to the creative woman who contributed to the art work in this deck to call it only the Rider-Waite deck. A. E. Waite was the creator of the ideas for the cards but Pamela Colman Smith designed the images. Rider was the name of the company that published them. Why is Mrs. Smith's name not mentioned? I prefer to call this deck the Waite-Smith deck. Though both the Crowley deck and the Waite-Smith deck have great wisdom within them, I have chosen to use a different deck in connection with this book. The deck I have chosen is called the Quest Tarot deck created by Joseph Ernest Martin.

Table A.1 - Minor Arcana Deck Comparison

Waite-Smith		Thoth		Quest	
Ace of Pentacles		Ace of Disks		Ace of Stones	abundance
2 of Pentacles		2 of Disks	change	2 of Stones	harmony
3 of Pentacles		3 of Disks	works	3 of Stones	work
4 of Pentacles		4 of Disks	power	4 of Stones	power of the earth
5 of Pentacles		5 of Disks	worry	5 of Stones	material difficulty
6 of Pentacles		6 of Disks	success	6 of Stones	success
7 of Pentacles		7 of Disks	failure	7of Stones	failure
8 of Pentacles		8 of Disks	prudence	8 of Stones	knowledge
9 of Pentacles		9 of Disks	gain	9 of Stones	material gain
10 of Pentacles		10 of Disks	wealth	10 of Stones	richness
Ace of Swords		Ace of Swords		Ace of Swords	cognition
2 of Swords		2 of Swords	peace	2 of Swords	peace
3 of Swords		3 of Swords	sorrow	3 of Swords	mourning
4 of Swords		4 of Swords	truce	4 of Swords	truce
5 of Swords		5 of Swords	defeat	5 of Swords	defeat
6 of Swords		6 of Swords	science	6 of Swords	science
7 of Swords		7 of Swords	futility	7 of Swords	uselessness
8 of Swords		8 of Swords	interference	8 of Swords	interference

Waite-Smith		Thoth		Quest	
9 of Swords		9 of Swords	cruelty	9 of Swords	cruelty
10 of Swords		10 of Swords	ruin	10 of Swords	ruin
Ace of Wands		Ace of Wands		Ace of Wands	passion
2 of Wands		2 of Wands	dominion	2 of Wands	dominion
3 of Wands		3 of Wands	virtue	3 of Wands	virtue
4 of Wands		4 of Wands	completion	4 of Wands	perfection
5 of Wands		5 of Wands	strife	5 of Wands	defeat
6 of Wands		6 of Wands	victory	6 of Wands	victory
7 of Wands		7 of Wands	valour	7 of Wands	courage
8 of Wands		8 of Wands	swiftness	8 of Wands	swiftness
9 of Wands		9 of Wands	strength	9 of Wands	power
10 of Wands		10 of Wands	oppression	10 of Wands	oppression
Ace of Cups		Ace of Cups		Ace of Cups	emotion
2 of Cups		2 of Cups	love	2 of Cups	love
3 of Cups		3 of Cups	abundance	3 of Cups	overflowing
4 of Cups		4 of Cups	luxury	4 of Cups	mixed emotions
5 of Cups		5 of Cups	disappointment	5 of Cups	disappointment
6 of Cups		6 of Cups	pleasure	6 of Cups	happiness
7 of Cups		7 of Cups	debauch	7 of Cups	illusions of success
8 of Cups		8 of Cups	indolence	8 of Cups	failure
9 of Cups		9 of Cups	happiness	9 of Cups	fortune

Waite-Smith		Thoth		Quest	
10 of Cups		10 of Cups	satiety	10 of Cups	success

Table A.2 - Court Card Deck Comparison

Waite-Smith		Thoth		Quest	
King of Pentacles		King of Disks		Mother of Stones	perception
Queen of Pentacles		Queen of Disks		Father of Stones	guardian
Knight of Pentacles		Knight of Disks		Daughter of Stones	possibilities
Page of Pentacles		Page of Disks		Son of Stones	advocate
King of Swords		King of Swords		Mother of Swords	mystery
Queen of Swords		Queen of Swords		Father of Swords	leadership
Knight of Swords		Knight of Swords		Daughter of Swords	confidence
Page of Swords		Page of Swords		Son of Swords	fairness
King of Wands		King of Wands		Mother of Wands	creator
Queen of Wands		Queen of Wands		Father of Wands	intelligence
Knight of Wands		Knight of Wands		Daughter of Wands	luxury
Page of Wands		Page of Wands		Son of Wands	charisma
King of Cups		King of Cups		Mother of Cups	motherhood

Waite-Smith		Thoth		Quest	
Queen of Cups		Queen of Cups		Father of Cups	fatherhood
Knight of Cups		Knight of Cups		Daughter of Cups	connection
Page of Cups		Page of Cups		Son of Cups	seeker

Table A. 3 - Major Arcana Deck Comparison

Waite-Smith		Thoth		Quest	
0 The Fool		0 The Fool		0 The Fool	beginnings
I The Magician		I The Magus		I The Magician	transmutation
II The High Priestess		II The Priestess		II The High Priestess	meditation
III The Empress		III The Empress		III The Empress	femininity
IV The Emperor		IV The Emperor		IV The Emperor	establishment
V Hierophant		V The Hierophant		V Hierophant	tradition
VI The Lovers		VI The Lovers		VI The Lovers	relationship
VII The Chariot		VII The Chariot		VII Chariot	willpower
VIII Strength		VIII Adjustment		VIII Strength	confidence
IX The Hermit		IX The Hermit		IX The Hermit	reflection
X Wheel of Fortune		X Fortune		X The Wheel of Fortune	chance

Waite-Smith		Thoth		Quest	
XI Justice		XI Lust		XI Justice	balance
XII The Hanged Man		XII The Hanged Man		XII The Hanged Man	uniqueness
XIII Death		XIII Death		XIII Death	endings
XIV Temperance		XIV Art		XIV Alchemy	restraint
XV The Devil		XV The Devil		XV The Devil	temptation
XVI The Tower		XVI The Tower		XVI The Tower	demolition
XVII The Star		XVII The Star		XVII The Star	hope
XVIII The Moon		XVIII The Moon		XVIII The Moon	dreams
XIX The Sun		XIX The Sun		XIX The Sun	life
XX Judgement		XX The Aeon		XX Aeon	rebirth
XXI The World		XXI The Universe		XXI The Universe	oneness
				0 The Multiverse	unbound
				blank card	

I have decided to use the Quest deck because of its amazing versatility. Not only does it have the standard cards used in almost all Tarot systems, it also has a wealth of additional information on each card. Embedded within the deck are features that allow you to answer yes/no questions, pursue questions about time, and identify physical characteristics about people. Its cards contain symbols of the I-Ching, the Elder Futhark Runes, Hebrew letters, astrological symbols, and letters of the alphabet. I also like the addition of the Multiverse and blank cards. The Multiverse card is really another 0 card like the Fool card symbolizing the the complete cycle made after the Fool has returned past the World or Universe card. Some decks have a blank or void card. In the book accompanying the Quest deck, Martin suggests using the blank card to create a personal card for your deck. I prefer to leave the card blank to represent the void - the mysterious everything/nothingness that precedes existence. It is not my aim to describe to you how to use any of these systems or special cards nor it it necessary for you to own this particular deck to do any of the exercises in this book. We will be doing activities that can be adapted for use with any standard Tarot deck.

I have divided the book into nine chapters each of which represents the seven planets and the realm of the stars as well as the introductory chapter on how to read the cards. Each subsequent chapter will focus on some of the particular influences of each planet and will offer interesting techniques for exploring those influences through the use of the Tarot cards. Each chapter except Chapter One (How To Read the Cards) and Chapter Eight (The Realm of the Stars) has ten exercises for each related planet. The following chart lists the seven planets and their influences used in this book.

Table A.4 – The Seven Planets

Planet	Influences
Sun	Self-expression, Health, Improving the self
Moon	Dreams, Dreamwork, Magick
Mercury	The Mind, Communication, Counseling, Meditation
Venus	Love, Relationships, Harmony, The Arts
Mars	Energy, Games, Fun, Sex
Jupiter	Expansion, Philosophy, Divination
Saturn	Limitation, Perseverance, Health, Time
Stars	New Possibilities

What I am calling the seven planets are, of course, those objects that were once thought of as the heavenly bodies that circled

Earth. Ancient philosophy once believed that when we were about to be born on Earth, our souls traveled from the realm of the stars through seven spheres of influence each dominated by a planet until that soul reached Earth and was born. As the soul passed through each sphere, it was influenced by the characteristics of the planet that ruled that sphere. The strength and type of influence was determined by the position of the planet within its sphere as the soul passed through it. The purpose of an astrological natal (birth) chart is to determine exactly how each planet influenced us as our souls made their way to Earth just before we were born. The Tarot, too, has its own universe. Each card is only a card until you influence it with your thoughts and energy. We determine what each card represents and, thus, give birth to its own unique characteristics. Any card can represent whatever you wish it to be. Once you begin working with a card and establishing its meaning, it will begin to take on those characteristics in your readings of that card. The mystery of the cards is that they signify nothing until you give them meaning – until you give them life. We will use the significance of the planets and several different activities to give the cards new uses and meanings.

In this text you will find new and interesting card spreads; games exclusively for the Tarot; ways to explore who you are; ideas for ritual and magick; ideas for meditation; suggestions on how to explore relationships; ways to be creative with the cards; ideas for how to use the cards to have better sex; suggestions on how to explore your own spiritual growth, health, and well being; and a whole host of other interesting ways to use the cards. In each chapter, we will explore at least two characteristics of each planet and how those characteristic can be explored through the cards with several different activities. These activities will come in four different varieties: spreads, discoveries, correspondences, and games. Many of you will already be familiar with card *spreads*. They are patterns of cards lain out on a table. Each of the cards in the various positions of the spread represent something in relation to the other cards. Together, the entire spread is used to derive a total reading of the cards. In a *discovery*, you will be using the cards as a guide to discover something about yourself or the world. A *correspondence* allows you to assign specific meanings or choices to the cards so that the cards can be used to choose an answer for you from several possibilities. Most often the

Major Arcana cards are used in correspondences. A *game* is an activity that involves using the cards for play – usually with others.

Each activity contains detailed instructions. In many cases, the activities, especially spreads, will also contain a sample reading to give you an idea on how the activity actually works. All the sample readings in this book were done as instructed in the activity giving me quite a few new insights along the way. Many of the instructions use the words "choose" and "pull" when describing how to pick cards. Each of these words has a different meaning in this book. When the word "pull" is used, it means to take a card from the deck in whatever random manner you have chosen to use. This means that you can pick the top card in the deck after shuffling or you can use another method for selecting cards. One method I often use is to place my sending hand (the power hand) on the deck and concentrate on sending energy into the deck while also focusing on my question or objective. Then I spread the cards out in on the table in a long row. With my receiving hand (the other hand) I feel the energy of the cards by slowly moving my hand above the cards until I feel one call to me. I then pull that card from the rest. To "choose" a card means to turn the cards face up and look through them until you find one that has the qualities you seek. An example of a card that may need to be chosen is the significator. This is a card which can be used to represent a person. In some cases, readers prefer to put a card in the center of their reading which closely represents the querent (the person seeking answers from the Tarot). Instead of pulling this card randomly, it is often necessary to search the cards to find the perfect representation.

How To Use This Book

There are several ways to use this book. The standard way, of course, is to read it from cover to cover and do all the exercises in the order they appear. This is a very fine way to read any book and you would get the full breadth of all the different uses of the Tarot demonstrated within, but there are other ways to use this book as well. A second way would to focus on a particular issue or concern that you may have in this time of your life. For example, if you are seeking to find a new relationship or you need to work on a current relationship, you may want to begin with the chapter entitled Venus and Love. If you are seeking ways of improving yourself, you may want to begin with the chapter entitled the Sun and Self. Yet another way to use this book would be to go to the chapter of a particular planet during the time when the moon enters the sign under the influence of that planet. For example, when the moon is full and rises in the house of Capricorn, you may want to go to the chapter on Saturn since Saturn rules the sign of Capricorn and then select an exercise from that chapter. In this way, you could make one of these Tarot activities part of each of your full moon rituals. Below are listed all the planets and their houses of influence. Since I am using only the original seven planets, I am not including Neptune, Uranus, or Pluto

Table A.5 Planets and Activities

Sign	Planet	Activity
Aries	Mars	an exercise from chapter five
Taurus	Venus	an exercise from chapter four
Gemini	Mercury	an exercise from chapter three
Cancer	Moon	an exercise from chapter two
Leo	Sun	an exercise from chapter one
Virgo	Mercury	an exercise from chapter three
Libra	Venus	an exercise from chapter four
Scorpio	Mars	an exercise from chapter five
Sagittarius	Jupiter	an exercise from chapter six
Capricorn	Saturn	an exercise from chapter seven
Aquarius	Saturn	an exercise from chapter seven
Pisces	Jupiter	an exercise from chapter six

Yet another way would be to use the entire Tarot deck to choose a specific exercise from the book. There are seven chapters with 10 activities and one chapter with eight activities totaling 78 activities. By choosing one Tarot card and referring to the numbered chart below, the cards can be used to randomly choose an exercise. After pulling a card, refer to the chart below to view the related activity number. A complete list of activities is listed in the appendix of this book.

Table A.6 Card Numbers

Number	Card	Number	Card
1	Ace of Stones	41	Mother of Stones
2	2 of Stones	42	Father of Stones
3	3 of Stones	43	Daughter of Stones
4	4 of Stones	44	Son of Stones
5	5 of Stones	45	Mother of Swords
6	6 of Stones	46	Father of Swords
7	7of Stones	47	Daughter of Swords
8	8 of Stones	48	Son of Swords
9	9 of Stones	49	Mother of Wands
10	10 of Stones	50	Father of Wands
11	Ace of Swords	51	Daughter of Wands
12	2 of Swords	52	Son of Wands
13	3 of Swords	53	Mother of Cups
14	4 of Swords	54	Father of Cups
15	5 of Swords	55	Daughter of Cups
16	6 of Swords	56	Son of Cups
17	7 of Swords	57	The Fool
18	8 of Swords	58	The Magician
19	9 of Swords	59	The High Priestess
20	10 of Swords	60	The Empress
21	Ace of Wands	61	The Emperor
22	2 of Wands	62	The Hierophant
23	3 of Wands	63	The Lovers
24	4 of Wands	64	The Chariot

Number	Card	Number	Card
25	5 of Wands	65	Strength
26	6 of Wands	66	The Hermit
27	7 of Wands	67	The Wheel of Fortune
28	8 of Wands	68	Justice
29	9 of Wands	69	The Hanged Man
30	10 of Wands	70	Death
31	Ace of Cups	71	Alchemy
32	2 of Cups	72	The Devil
33	3 of Cups	73	The Tower
34	4 of Cups	74	The Star
35	5 of Cups	75	The Moon
36	6 of Cups	76	The Sun
37	7 of Cups	77	Aeon
38	8 of Cups	78	The Universe
39	9 of Cups		
40	10 of Cups		

One tried and true method for discovery with the cards is by doing card spreads. Almost all Tarot books list at least one spread. There are also several books with a wide range of interesting spreads. This book will provide you with many new and interesting spreads but each will have a specific which will go beyond the traditional process of trying to read "the future." It should be noted that all exercises in this book are designed for exploration. Feel free to change and use them for yourself to make each work best for you. I recommend that you try the spread as it is explained and then experiment with alterations. Some ways to explore alternatives are to: change the function of certain positions or add more positions, use different decks with the same spreads, use doublings or reversals, or add other tools to the reading. A doubling is done when you place additional cards one top of a card already placed in a spread. Doubling allows you to obtain additional information about a particular position or card. Usually, not all cards within a spread are doubled (unless, of course, the spread calls for that). Doubling is mostly used when a particular card seems confusing or inadequate to answer the question and the reader feels that an additional card is needed to amplify or clarify the information given by the original card. Other tools can be used in conjunction with the cards. One of my first Tarot teachers used rune stones that he placed on each card to amplify its meaning. If a certain position or definition of a position within a spread does not speak to you then change it to suit your needs. Whatever method or procedures you choose should work well within the whole spread and help to illuminate the chosen goal or theme for the reading. Additional positions can be included with any spread but, again, should be done in order to amplify or clarify the overall reading.

Readings can also be altered by the use of different Tarot decks; there are so many varied and interesting decks out there. Each one is sure to give one spread different meanings and nuances to a reading. If you have several decks, try using each in the same spread and compare the readings. There is always a controversy about reading reversed (upside-down) cards. You should decide for yourself whether or not you wish to use reversals and the meanings they may provide to your readings.

No matter which way you choose to use this book, I hope you will feel free to explore the universe of possibilities with your cards and that you will have fun in the process - which brings me to another point. This book is about having fun. There are already plenty of serious books about Tarot out there. Tarot can be a very serious study, indeed, but it does not have to only be about quietly unlocking the mysteries of the universe in some darkly lit study. One of the mysteries of the universe is to learn how to go through life with joy. Some of the exercises in this book will be about self discovery and learning but there also exercises which are designed just for having fun. By all means, I hope this book will help you take yourself and others seriously - but not too seriously! Enjoy your journey with the cards into the universe of new possibilities!

A Brief Explanation of the Chapters

In Chapter One: *The Sun and the Self,* you will explore who you are and how you can better become who you are. This is the stuff of traditional Tarot readings but I have added some new and interesting ideas such as discovering your Tarot personality and then using that information to learn how you can better deal with others in your life. With Chapter Two: *The Moon and Magick,* we take a look at how you can perform magick and do other methods of deep work with Tarot. The symbolism in the cards is an excellent tool for use with visualization and representations. This chapter also helps you learn to better interpret your dreams and offers you some unique methods for practicing meditation. Chapter Three: *Mercury and the Mind* deals with the two ways that information can flow - in through learning and out through communication. The exercises in learning help you to focus on what we need to know while the exercises in communication help us learn to express your thoughts and feelings to others.

Chapter Four: *Venus and Love* offers you some ways to help develop and strengthen all the many relationships you have with other people. The chapter also deals with another form of passion which is expressed through the arts. Tarot offers some very unique ways to inspire us to create and express works of art. Chapter Five: *Mars and Energy* takes into account the powerful energies represented by the planet Mars. You will observe how to use the energy of Earth. You will also learn to better use one of the strongest energies of the universe - the energy of sexuality. Finally, the chapter will offer some ways to use your own energy to have fun through games and sports. In Chapter Six: *Jupiter and Transcendence,* you will be introduced with the more mysterious energies of the universe through developing your spiritual side and your own powers of divination. In this section you learn how to combine Tarot with other methods of spiritual learning and divination. Chapter Seven: *Saturn and Limitations* uses the powers of Saturn to explore limitations. Physical limitations are often defined by health. This chapter will help you examine your physical strength and offer guidance in learning how to strengthen yourself. The chapter will also look at the physical limitations of the universe which we experience through space and time. Beyond the physical, you will also explore limitations of the mind, the heart, and the soul. Chapter Eight: *The Stars and New Possibilities* brings you beyond the ancient seven planet solar system into the mysterious sphere beyond which holds the bright jewels of the night sky we call stars. This chapter will include ways to help you learn your own cards and will teach you some new general divination spreads.

The Appendices contain a wealth of information as well. The first appendix contains 14 new and fun games for use exclusively with Tarot cards. The remaining appendices list all the different activities through out the book for easy reference.

Chapter 1

Down to Earth: How to Read the Cards

Introduction

any books written on the topic of Tarot cards and the pamphlets that come with most new Tarot card decks describe how to read the cards and how to create and read spreads with the cards. Mostly, though, the meanings of the cards are derived from the art work and images on each card. This, of course, is a fine way to understand each card but the meanings described in this manner make each deck unique. The reader becomes dependent on the art work for interpretation and completely different meanings can result from the use of different tarot decks. I like to teach a system that is not solely dependent on the art work but seeks meaning from all the information provided by each card. By using this system, the meanings of cards can be determined quickly without depending on the particular images used in each individual deck. I am not suggesting that you should ignore the images portrayed on cards, rather, I am recommending that those images be used as just one source of information. The images, combined with the other information on the cards such as the suit and the numbers can provide a wealth of information to card readers.

I suggest that, when learning the Tarot, a few key words or phrases be memorized for each card. With a minimum of 78 cards, learning a few words for each card is a large task in and of itself. Key words can help you to quickly determine a possible meaning for a card but, as you become more experienced with reading the Tarot, you should work to go beyond those key words until they are no longer needed and many unique interpretations for each card are possible. Though many students resist this idea, it must be remembered that no card ever has a single meaning every time it is used. One card alone can have many meanings and the interpretation of that card should depend upon all the information available on the card as well as information learned about the querent, the particular situation, the spread, and the intuition of the reader. Furthermore, cards take on the meanings instilled upon them by their user and can change as the reader changes. A book about Tarot cards (including this one) should never be the sole source of information about any card. That being said, this chapter will help beginning or novice learn to read their cards regardless of what deck is being used. This information should be only a starting point for a long journey of learning and experience with the Tarot.

The standard Tarot deck has at least 78 cards. The cards are divided into three categories. The Major Arcana is the name of the category of cards that contain a number and at least one word. The numbers range from 0 to 21. Many of the Major Arcana such as the Lovers and the Hanged Man are traditional while others can differ from deck to deck. Many decks use capital Roman numerals to differentiate the Major Arcana from the Minor Arcana. The Minor Arcana cards usually have Arabic numerals from Ace (1) - 10. There are four suits for the Minor Arcana much like there are four suits and numbers used for a standard deck of 52 playing cards. The names of these suits can differ. The traditional names are disks, wands, rods, and cups. The last category of cards are called the Court cards because they usually contain images of human figures with names such as the King, Queen, Princess, Knight, and other members of a royal court. The Court cards also use the same four suits as the Minor Arcana. The Court Cards can be similar to the courtly figures familiar in standard playing cards.

Reading the Minor Arcana

The Minor Arcana cards contain a number and a suit. The four suits are related to the four elements: Earth, Air, Fire, and Water. The meanings of each of these elements can be related directly to the cards.

Table 1.1 Suit Correspondences

Suit	Element	Correspondence	Keyword
Stones (Disks)	Earth	financial, business, physical health	physical
Swords	Air	thinking, communication, mental health, visualization	mental
Wands	Fire	relationships, life energy, emotional health	emotional
Cups	Water	inner emotions, connections, inner strength	spiritual

The element Earth represents our physical bodies and the material world around us. This includes the things that we come in contact with in our daily lives including our work, finances, and all aspects of the material world. The element of Air represents our mental abilities and interactions with others. All actions involving the mind and the need to communicate our ideas to others are part of this element. Fire represents the emotional side of ourselves. Fire is energy and our emotions are often the source of energy that motivates us to do many things. That energy is experienced within ourselves and between others. Water is related to the spiritual or how we are connected to the universe and all things. Our view of the world and how it works will be directly reflected through our image of ourselves and through how we act in the world.

The numbers of the Minor Arcana represent a story of the creation of the universe. 1 (represented by the Ace) is the number of the beginning where all things start as one thing. From this eternal unity comes the division that eventually manifests into the myriad of things we experience in existence, including ourselves. That final manifestation is represented by the numbers 9 and 10.

Table 1.2 Number Correspondences

Number	The Story of Creation	Correspondence	Keyword
1 (Ace)	The one comes into existence.	beginning, purity	source
2	The one divides into opposites.	division, separation	change
3	The two create life.	reunion, balance, birth, short travel	creation
4	A home is created for life.	foundations, meetings	home
5	Humankind is created but ignorance creates loss.	cycles, sorrow, humanity	loss
6	Humankind learns about its source.	learning, insight, gain, expansion	exploration
7	Humankind discovers personal and spiritual love.	spirituality, luck, love, philosophy	mystery
8	Death/rebirth is created for change and renewal.	infinity, cycle of birth/death, health	rebirth
9	Creation and learning is accomplished.	completion, ending, resolution	accomplishment
10	A new direction in creation and learning begins.	a new start, transcendence	commitment

The number one represents the single source of all life and for all things (which I call Spirit). It can be symbolized by the point or circle. In order for the source to experience itself, it moves and divides to create the masculine and feminine energies that are part of everything. I call these energies God and Goddess and they are represented by the number two. These two energies produce a third neutral energy which is the potential for all life. I call this energy the Child and it is represented by the number three. In order for life to manifest, it must have a place to exist - a home. Through the potential for creation made possible by the God, Goddess, and Child, the four elements come into existence to create all the matter and material existence needed for life. Finally, life itself becomes possible which is represented by the number 5. That number is abundant in the human figure. Unfortunately, life is born into existence without the knowledge of its own source. Many creatures come to this understanding naturally and intuitively but mankind is one that does not. In order to live fully, mankind must come to know the source of life and the spiritual reality of one's existence. Therefore, at least in the Tarot, five represents sorrow or a loss. The path that leads back to Spirit is described in the progression of the Major Arcana cards but the remaining numbers describe how creation becomes manifest and complete.

In order for mankind to return to Spirit, there must take place exploration and learning. This process is part of the cycle of life; all people must learn how to live their lives with meaning and that process is represented by the number six - the number of exploration. People must eventually come to terms with the mystery of life and its source and that is the learning objective suggested by the number 6. That mystery is represented by the number seven which combines the number three (the spiritual triad) with the number four (the material square). Seven represents that which must be learned. Eight represents the cosmic cycles of life and death. Through it we learn that all things must end and be renewed. Rather than being frightened by death, one can learn to live life fully knowing that life is finite yet one can also take some comfort in knowing that all things become new again. Through death, life returns to its source so that new life can be possible again. Nine represents the completion of the cycle of creation but Eight has taught us that there is no such thing as a true ending. The cycle of creation is not a straight line with a final ending. Ten represents that all learning and living happens in spirals and not straight lines. When the cycle of creation appears to have ended, it simply begins again at a higher level for 10 is nothing but 1 at a new dimension symbolized by the addition of a zero.

By combining the keywords of the numbers with the suits, the following chart can be created. Remember that these keywords are only to be used as an aid to help remember some of the many meanings of each card. Be flexible when using them.

Table 1.3 The Minor Arcana

	Stones	Swords	Wands	Cups
Ace	Physical Source	Mental Source	Emotional Source	Spiritual Source
2	Physical Change	Mental Change	Emotional Change	Spiritual Change
3	Physical Creation	Mental Creation	Emotional Creation	Spiritual Creation
4	Physical Home	Mental Home	Emotional Home	Spiritual Home
5	Physical Loss	Mental Loss	Emotional Loss	Spiritual Loss
6	Physical Exploration	Mental Exploration	Emotional Exploration	Spiritual Exploration
7	Physical Mystery	Mental Mystery	Emotional Mystery	Spiritual Mystery
8	Physical Rebirth	Mental Rebirth	Emotional Rebirth	Spiritual Rebirth
9	Physical Accomplishment	Mental Accomplishment	Emotional Accomplishment	Spiritual Accomplishment
10	Physical Commitment	Mental Commitment	Emotional Commitment	Spiritual Commitment

Reading the Court Cards

The Court cards represent people in our lives that influence what we say and do. We are a social animal so there will always other people who will affect and be affected by our actions. The Court cards can help you to identify those people and understand their characteristics in relation to a particular situation. The Court cards continue to use the same four suits as the Minor Arcana but do not have numbers. Instead, these cards use the designation of 3 - 4 human figures.

Table 1.4 Court People

Card	Person
Daughter (Princess)	young female
Son (Prince)	young male
Father (King)	older male
Mother (Queen)	older female

The four suits create personality traits related to their respective elements.

Table 1.5 Court Personalities

Element	Keyword
Earth	Strong
Air	Intelligent
Fire	Passionate
Water	Spiritual

From these attributes we can derive a chart illustrating each Court card.

Table 1.6 Court Cards

	Stones	Swords	Wands	Cups
Daughter	Strong young woman	Intelligent young woman	Passionate young woman	Spiritual young woman
Son	Strong young man	Intelligent young man	Passionate young man	Spiritual young man
Father	Strong older man	Intelligent older man	Passionate older man	Spiritual older man
Mother	Strong older woman	Intelligent older woman	Passionate older woman	Spiritual older woman

There are times when the Court cards indicate something that has the quality of the type of person indicated without actually relating to a specific human individual. The Daughter of Stones, for example, can represent a person who is a strong young woman or it may represent another creature or situation that might resemble the characteristics of a strong young woman. The specific meaning can be made clear in the context of the reading and the specific situation being observed.

Reading the Major Arcana

The Major Arcana cards represent the qualities needed for taking on the spiritual journey from the place of sorrow brought upon by the ego centered life toward the fulfilled life of oneness with Spirit. The number 5 in the Minor Arcana tells the story of the creation of humankind where humanity is not immediately aware of its own spiritual source. The Major Arcana is the recipe for finding and returning to that source so that a life of spiritual significance can be discovered and led. The Major Arcana does not prescribe a specific journey for the spiritual path is different for every traveler; not everyone needs to follow the cards in exactly the same order. Instead, the cards describe certain qualities that are needed for a person to learn to connect and live with Spirit. There are, however, four major stages of development that are outlined in the progression of the

Major Arcana from 0 to 21, each of which is related to one of the four elements.

Table 1.7 Major Arcana Stages

Stage	Element	Focus	Cards
1	Earth	People	0 – VI
2	Air	Attitudes	VII – XI
3	Fire	Actions	XII – XVI
4	Water	Connections	XVII – XXI+

The first stage involves people in your life that will influence your progression in the path. In some cases, you will need to reconcile your differences with people and, in other cases, you will need to seek out certain people to help you along your way or you may need to discover the qualities of that person within yourself. The cards in this first stage (0 - VI) are all represented by human figures. The cards of the second stage deal with attitudes that need to be developed to move further along the path. The third stage describes specific actions that need to be taken to break from conventional and personal bounds that prevent you from seeking Spirit and the fourth stage describes those things with which you will need to find a personal connection in order learn to let go and become one with all things - the goal of seeking Spirit.

Table 1.8 Major Arcana

No.	Name	Path	Stage	Keyword
0	Fool	The person who commits	1	Beginning
I	Magician	The person of possibilities	1	Masculine
II	Priestess	The person who affirms	1	Feminine
III	Empress	The earthly feminine	1	Mother
IV	Emperor	The earthly masculine	1	Father
V	Hierophant	The person who gives lessons	1	Teacher
VI	Lovers	The person who loves	1	Love
VII	Chariot	Willing to find the path	2	Path
VIII	Strength	Willing to push on	2	Strength
IX	Hermit	Willing to find answers from within	2	Contemplation
X	Wheel of Fortune	Willing to accept change	2	Flexibility
XI	Justice	Willing to accept others	2	Justice
XII	Hanged Man	Act in the service of others	3	Sacrifice
XIII	Death	Spiritually dying to a new life	3	Rebirth
XIV	Alchemy	Learning about creativity	3	Art
XV	Devil	Finding humor	3	Trickster
XVI	Tower	Overcoming old ways	3	Innovation
XVII	Star	Connecting with the creative force	4	Being
XVIII	Moon	Connecting with the unifying force	4	Belonging
XIX	Sun	Connecting with the dividing force	4	Becoming
XX	Aeon	Connecting with time	4	Patience
XXI	Universe	Connecting with space	4	Wholeness
0	Multiverse	Connecting with all things	4	Unity
(blank)	Void	Complete loss of the ego self	4	Selflessness

The path to spiritual awakening begins with the number 0 - The Fool. Learning to break away from the shackles of the desire driven ego often begins with a personal conflict - something that brings on sorrow. That conflict can cause you to look for solutions beyond the self and seek connections. It sometimes takes meeting someone who has had a similar experience and has learned to overcome it to find inspiration to overcome your sorrow. You may learn from this person personally or through their works (such as through books) and determine that you, too, will overcome your challenge and learn to become a better person. It is easy to simply go through the motions of life and conform to the norms and expectations of the culture. It appears foolish to others to break away from that, but true lasting happiness that is found only by connecting to the love and energy of the universe must be sought by setting out on your own. The story of creation set about by the Minor Arcana tells us that this seeking is what each of us is meant to do. The Fool leaps where others dare not go and, thus, the journey begins.

The Magician (I) lets you know that it is possible to change. He teaches you that things do not have to be the way they are and that a new reality can be created through the application of energy and desire coupled with work and perseverance. You may meet someone or learn from someone with these qualities or you may learn to develop them yourself and become the Magician. The High Priestess (II) helps us to affirm that you can indeed do the work that is ahead for you. She teaches that all people are worthy of finding their spiritual source. With the Empress (III) and the Emperor (IV), you must come to terms with your own mother and father and with those people in your life who have acted as mothers and fathers to you. In the process, you learn to develop your own mother and father qualities within yourself until you can become a nurturing and supporting person regardless of whether or not you experienced those things with your own parents or guardians. The Hierophant (V) is the teacher who gives you the actual lessons you need to get on your way. Almost all seekers need some kind of teaching in order to begin and many people begin their journey by reading a book that inspires them to explore a new path. The Teacher can only offer the lessons, however. It will be up to the student to do the work to learn and grow. Eventually, the student will go beyond the teacher and have to continue the walk alone. The Lover (VI) is the one who offers support and compassion without judgments. It helps to have a lover to support you through the difficult times of change but it is also important to learn to become the nonjudgmental lover for yourself and others. All major religious traditions teach that learning to become the Lover is a primary goal of the spiritual path.

In the second stage, the you learn to develop specific attitudes that help you in your spiritual goal. The Chariot (VII) encourages the seeker to be willing to accept a new path in life. The pursuit of the spiritual requires breaking away from certain cultural and personal habits and traditions. You will need to be willing to walk in unfamiliar territory and doing so requires an attitude of patience and fortitude. Going in a new direction also requires Strength (VIII) to be willing to walk the path against any and all forces that may try to prevent you from continuing. The Hermit (IX) asks you to find answers from within yourself and not just from without. Although you were asked to find a teacher earlier, it is important that you also look inside for answers. The Wheel of Fortune (X) teaches us that change is a constant in life. The spiritual path will be filled with different circumstances and you will need to be flexible and spontaneous to deal with those changes and continue being focused on the path. The Justice card (XI) asks you to accept others and to be fair and compassionate in your dealings with them. Others will be on their spiritual journeys at the same time as you will be on yours. In order to ask them to be respectful of your pursuit, you need to be willing to do the same for them.

The first two stages of the Major Arcana prepare you to be the kind of person that is needed to begin the pursuit of spiritual truth. In the third stage, you take on some specific actions to become a truly spiritual person. The Hanged Man (XII) asks you to make a sacrifice. When you make a sacrifice, you give up something that is important to you. One way to sacrifice is to give up time to help others. In doing so, you come to recognize the needs of others and begin to find your own desires to be less important. You also learn to see things through the eyes of others and can become less dogmatic and rigid in your own views. The Death card (XIII) asks you to kill off the old self so that a new one can be reborn. The initiation ceremonies of many religious traditions such as the those practiced as part of the Eleusian mysteries simulated a type of death and rebirth that made the initiates see the world in a new way - just as if they had been actually reborn. The seeker will need to find a way to simulate this type of awakening. Alchemy (XIV) asks you to engage in a creative act that will help you explore and express your inner feelings. The Alchemists of old used to transform raw materials into gold not through actual compounds but through the work of the soul. You will need to search out and bring to the surface the gold within your soul. The Devil (XV) reminds you to not always take yourself seriously. The spiritual path is meant to help you become a happier person and one quality of the happy person is that she knows how to laugh. Many become so serious in their spiritual pursuits that they forget to have fun and relax. The Devil is the trickster who looks for flaws and contradictions. He asks you to keep your eye open for these gaffs and learn to be light-hearted about them. The Tower (XVI) asks you to break from the traditions and rules of the culture and your past - not just in attitude but in action as well. At this point, you will need to "come out" and be open and honest about who you are and who you are becoming.

The final stage of the Major Arcana helps seek connections with the universe moving you from an ego-centered desire driven person into someone who becomes an equal part of all things. The ultimate spiritual goal is to dissolve yourself completely until you become immersed in Spirit. The Star (XVII)represents the neutral energy of the Child. That energy is creative and inspirational; it is the energy that makes life possible. With the Star, you are asked to connect to that universal creative energy I call the force of Life. When you have connected to that force, I say that you are in a state of Being. Being means that you live fully in the present moment without any desires to be something or someone else. The Star is also about hope. The end of the struggle is near and now is the time to gather one last burst of hopeful anticipation to make it to the end. The Moon (XVIII) asks you to connect to the feminine energy of the universe - the force that combines all things and brings us together. That force is the universal energy of Love. When you are connected to that force, I call it Belonging. In a state of Belonging, you feel personally related to the entire universe and experience a universal sense of contentment and love. The Sun (XIX) relates to the force that makes us each individual beings. I call that the force of Light and experiencing it is called

Becoming. Through this energy you learn about exactly who you are and become the person you were meant to be. This may sound like an opposition to the goal of releasing the self from the bonds of ego control but there is a difference between selfishness and self-full-ness. The self-full person has the confidence and self knowledge that allows her to seek only what she needs, express herself in positive ways, and find ways to use her strengths to help make the world a better place. Aeon (XX) asks us to connect to the concept of time. In our daily lives, time feels like a constraint and limitation but the truth of the universe is that time is actually fluid and eternal. We think in terms of straight lines - everything has a beginning and an ending - but the universe knows only cycles and circles. Time is just one way to keep those cycles going - timelessly. When we connect with time, we can learn to stop fearing it and, in so doing, develop patience. The Universe card (XXI) calls us to connect with another universal constant - space itself. When you connect with the vastness of space you realize how small you really are though you do not feel insignificant because you have come to learn that everything in space has its own worth. The smallest one-celled creature is no less significant and important to the universe than is an entire solar system of planets and creatures. Through the Universe card, you become connected to all things equally.

The standard Tarot deck usually has 21 cards in its Major Arcana but the Quest deck has two additional cards so I will discuss them here. The Multiverse card (0) is meant to illustrate the cyclic nature of spiritual growth. No one ever completely finishes learning and growing spiritually. It is impossible to completely become totally united with Spirit and also maintain a strong self identity that is needed to survive on a daily basis but that fact is not a reason to stop trying. The irony of the spiritual journey is that the more you learn to break away from the self and connect to Spirit, the more your individual life becomes fulfilling and meaningful. The Multiverse card recognizes the concept of multiple universes which gives our universe an endless range of possibilities. Through these possibilities, you are able to find new ideas and concepts to explore which can enrich your spiritual understanding of life and the universe even more. The Void card asks you to try and grasp a difficult concept - that of the emptiness or complete nothingness of the universe. It is hard for us to understand such a concept since we do not experience total nothingness. At this level, we enter the world of the paradox for the Void is both nothing and everything; it is the essence of the energy of Spirit. If you can come to understand this seemingly impossible concept then you can understand some of the great mysteries of the universe.

Fluency with the Cards

The next step in learning to read the cards is to simply practice, practice, practice. I suggest that you put your cards into the order listed for each of the three sections that have been discussed in this chapter. Put your Minor Arcana cards in order from Ace to 10 in each of the four suits. Go through the cards while you study the story of the creation of the universe and the influence of each element. Memorize the keywords for each card keeping in mind that additional meanings for each card will also become evident the more you work with them. Put your Court cards in order within each suit. Memorize the qualities of each personality and the influence of each element on those personalities. Put your Major Arcana cards in order from 0 to 21 (or more) and study the spiritual path that it describes.

When you have finished learning the keywords, I suggest that you shuffle your cards and randomly pull one at a time using that card as a source for meditation. Connect with the card and let everything on that card - the numbers, the elements, the words, and the images - speak to you until you feel you have a personal understanding of the many possibilities of that card. The next step in learning is to begin to try some simple spreads and learn how to read inter-connections between the cards. You can start with just two or three cards and practice creating a situation or story that is revealed by them. Chapter 10 of this book gives you some ideas for ways to practice reading the cards and offers some interesting spreads to learn and try.

Chapter 2

The Sun and Self

Introduction

he sun is the most observable, brightest, and most influential of all the seven "planets" in our solar system. It provides all life on Earth with warmth, light, and the energy needed to live and grow. Without the sun we would all die. With such awesome power and control over life it is only reasonable to honor the sun as a great provider. We, of course, only experience the direct influence of the sun for about half the time of each day. For most people, the daytime is when they are out and about leading active lives. The sun, then, represents the active self - the part of each of us that interacts with others. The sun represents how we express ourselves. It also represents our general state of health which is an indication of our life force and how well our natural energies are flowing. With the influence of the sun, we can determine how to understand and improve ourselves. In this chapter, we will explore how to use the Tarot to discover who you are and how you can learn to fully be yourself.

Discovering Who You Are

1. Discovering Your Personality
(a spread)

In this spread you will discover how you actually appear to others and compare that to your own sense of self. You will also be given information on how you can balance these two concepts or find a way to bridge the gap between them. Search the entire deck for a card that best represents your own image of who you are. Be as honest as you can be with yourself. Then, shuffle the deck and pull another card. This card will represent how you actually appear to others. If there is a great difference between the two, a third card will help reveal how you can find a way to better bridge the second card with the first or, if the second card is read as an undesirable trait, the third card can tell you how to avoid that impression. The third card can also be used to show how you can balance the first and second cards.

Purpose: To discover who you really are.

Procedure:
1. Choose the first card to represent yourself.
2. Pull two additional cards.
3. Lay the cards out in this pattern.

Drawing 1

Representations:
1. Your personality
2. How you actually appear to others
3. A bridge or balance between the two

Sample Reading:
1. IX The Hermit
2. XIX The Sun
3. 0 The Multiverse

I chose the Hermit card to represent myself. I am mostly a very shy and withdrawn person and being alone to study and write is my idea of a great time. I am very much a hermit at heart though I do occasionally enjoy being out with a few friends. The Hermit card best represents that side of myself and reflects much of what makes up my personality. The Sun card is the card I pulled to represent how I appear to others. In the Quest deck, the Sun represents life and strong energy. This is very different than the card I chose to represent myself. The cards seem to say that that I appear much more lively to others in their presence than I thought. The third card, the bridge card, is the Multiverse card. This is a card unique to the Quest deck. It represents a step beyond the 21st card of the Major Arcana while also being a card that can be placed before the Fool card. It is a connection between the end and the beginning of the Major Arcana thus creating a true cycle. I read this card as meaning that I need to find balance between my hermit self and my appearance to others. Being locked up in room all my life will not do well for my whole being. I will need to be both an introvert and an extrovert to become the person I was meant to be.

2. Elemental Strengths
(a spread)

This spread will help you determine where your particular strengths and weaknesses are at the present time. It may help you to approach a particular challenge by focusing on your current strengths or by working on a particular weakness. You will first shuffle your deck and then draw a number of cards until you reach your first Stones (Disks) card. The more cards it takes for you to reach that card indicates a growing weakness in that area. You will then do the same for all the other elements or suits.

Purpose: To determine your own strengths and weaknesses according to related elements.

Procedure:
1. Earth: Shuffle the deck and set it down. Flip over the top card and continue to flip cards until you turn over a Stones or Disks card. Count how many cards it took you to reach that card and make a note. Do not count the final card - that you will keep. After finishing, place the other cards back into the deck. The number of cards turned over represents your current material strength. (Less is stronger). The card revealed is the current material lesson needed.
2. Do the same procedure three more times for each suit and

place the cards in the following spread.

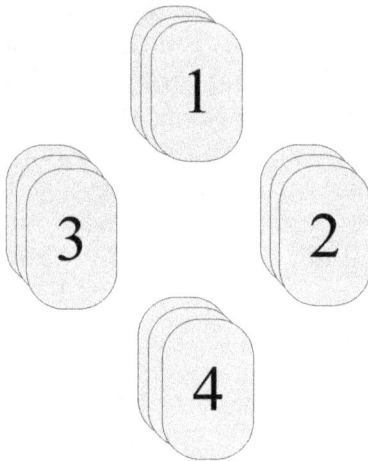

Drawing 2

Representations:
1. Current material strength and lesson needed.
2. Mental lesson and strength.
3. Emotional lesson and strength.
4. Spiritual lesson and strength.

Sample Reading:
1. Son of Stones (21 cards)
2. Daughter of Swords (3 cards)
3. Four of Wands (2 cards)
4. Four of Cups (6 cards)

Clearly, my weakest area in this reading is in the material. It took 21 cards to reach a Stones card for the element of Earth while it only took 6 or less cards to find the other elemental cards. This would indicate that I need to concentrate on the material part of my life in order to strengthen it. How to do that is indicated by the card that I reached. In the Quest deck, the Son of Stones represents the advocate or the person who stands up for another person in times of trouble. Since one attribute of the material is work, I will need to be on the lookout for who will need me to stand up for them at work. By doing so, I will not only be helping someone else, I will be strengthening myself as well.

3. Discovering Your Fate
(a discovery)

This activity uses the divinatory tool of numerology which plays an important role in the Tarot. You will use only the Major Arcana cards to relate to numbers you derive from your birth date. To use the major arcana cards you will need to reduce numbers down until you get one that is less than 25. Most tarot decks have 22 major arcana cards if you count the Fool card as number 22. The Quest deck, however, has some additional cards including the 0 Multiverse card and the blank card I call the Void card. For that reason I assign the Multiverse card the number 23 and the Void card the number 24. If you use a different deck, you will need to establish correspondences to the numbers 23 and 24.

Each of these numbers relates also to sacred cycles that influence our lives. The Destiny Number correlates with your life cycle and is related to your life long destiny. The Day Number relates to Earth cycles or the day and explores how your destiny can be brought to life each day. The Month Number relates to moon cycles. The moon influences our inner dreams and desires so its number correlates to our inner and hidden influences that affect our destiny. The Year number relates to sun cycles. The sun represents your outer appearance to others. Its number determines influences upon your destiny from outside.

Purpose: To discover your fate and destiny in life by using the numbers associated with the Tarot. There will be several operations involved in this process.

Procedure:
1. The Destiny Number: Add together your full birth date to get a number less than 25. Compare that number to the Major Arcana card of the same number. The Destiny Number determines your destiny in life.
2. The Day Number: Add together the day of your birth to get a

number less than 25.Compare that number to the Major Arcana card of the same number. The Day Number determines how your destiny may be manifest.

3. The Month Number: Find out if you were born during the waning moon or the waxing moon. If you were born during the waxing moon compare your month number to the Major Arcana card of the same number. If you were born during the waning moon multiply your month number by 2 and compare that number to the corresponding Major Arcana card. The number 24 will be represented by the void card. If you do not know under which moon you were born compare both cards for the best answer. The Month Number determines the internal influences of your destiny.

4. The Year Number: Add together the numbers of your full birth year to get a number less than 25. Compare to the corresponding Major Arcana card. The Year Number determines the external influences of your destiny.

Sample Reading:

My birthday is December 22, 1959 which gives me the numbers 12, 22, 1959. Adding up 12 + 22 + 19 + 59, I get 112. To get a number less than 23, I will add 1+1+2 to get 4. Four is my destiny number. The Major Arcana IV card is the Emperor. In the Quest deck, that card stands for establishment and the Emperor is the earthly male figure. My destiny is to help establish something strong and material during my lifetime - something I am trying to do through my writing. My day number is 22 which is the 0 or Fool card. Therefore, my destiny will be manifest by not constantly worrying about what I want to do. I need to just jump right in and move forward. This I need to do on a daily basis. I was born during the waning moon of the 12th month giving me the number 24 which is the Void card. This means my internal influences cannot not truly be known and it is best not to try and discover them. The muse and my inspiration should remain a mystery. My year number is 24 which is also the Void card. It would seem that I am not to know what my influences nor should I try to explore them. It is best that I just write from the heart and go with the flow.

4. Fear and Inspiration
(a spread)

This spread helps you to understand what it is that causes you fear and inspiration either overall or in a particular situation. Fear and inspiration are like two poles on a battery. If there is something that you fear, you will do your best to avoid it. If, despite your best efforts, you do actually encounter your fear, that encounter will sap your energy. Conversely, things that inspire you give you energy and the will to act and create. In your life, it can help to understand what it is that drains you and what it is that energizes you. By balancing these two forces, you can learn to seek your inspiration in order to act and overcome your fears.

Purpose: To discover what your particular fear and inspiration may be and to determine how you can use the two to your advantage.

Procedure:
1. Pull three cards.
2. Lay the cards out in the following way.

```
      2

      3

      1
```
Drawing 3

Representations:
1. Your fear or that which absorbs your energy.
2. Your inspiration or that which gives you energy.
3. How to balance the two

Sample Reading:
1. Father of Wands

2. XVII The Star
3. Daughter of Swords

It would seem that I fear the emotional male figure (Father of Wands). That figure could be myself or someone else. I read it as being myself which means I have a fear of expressing emotions - a common malady for us Hermit types. My inspiration comes from my hopes and bits of wisdom that I collect along my path (The Star) and the way to seek that inspiration is to balance my fear of the emotional self by encouraging my understanding of my own inner feminine self (Daughter of Swords) which will help me discover those things that energize my hopes.

5. The Stages of Life
(a spread)

Each of the stages of your life provide unique challenges and opportunities for growth. There are four primary stages of life. These phases are the Child, the Maiden/Suitor, the Mother/Father, and the Crone/Sage periods in life. To learn what each phase of your life has or can teach you, choose cards in your deck that represent each phase. Then, randomly pull cards that provide insight on the actual meaning of these times. Carefully compare the two cards of each stage and let them teach you about yourself, your past, and your future. Obviously, depending on your age, you will have to project forward and determine how you may approach those stages.

Purpose: To understand yourself as you manifest through the different stages of life.

Procedure:
1. Choose a card that best represents the Child phase of your life (ages 1 – 14).
2. Choose a card that best represents the Maiden/ Suitor phase of your life (15 – 28).
3. Choose a card that best represents the Mother/ Father phase of your life (29 42).
4. Choose a card that best represents the Crone/ Sage phase of

your life (43 -).

5. Pull four more cards and place beside the first four in this pattern:

Drawing 4

1	5
2	6
3	7
4	8

Representations:
1. Your view of your Child phase
2. Your view of your Maiden/Suitor phase
3. Your view of your Mother/Father phase
4. Your view of your Crone/Sage phase
5. Your actual Child phase
6. Your actual Mother/Father phase
7. Your actual Crone/Sage phase

Sample Reading:
1. Five of Stones
2. XVII The Star
3. Eight of Stones
4. Son of Cups
5. Daughter of Wands
6. Ace of Swords

7. XV The Devil
8. 6 of Wands

I chose the Five of Stones to represent my Child phase because it was a time of physical difficulties for me as I spent much of my childhood going in and out of hospitals. Curiously, the actuality of that time according to my pulled card is that it was still a time of youthful energy. The Daughter of Wands card is identified as a card of luxury. Looking back on my childhood, I think back on how sitting and pondering in those hospital rooms gave me plenty of time to think and reflect so that I could become the inquisitive person that I am now. I chose the Star card to represent my Suitor phase because it was a time of great hope and expectation for me. I grew healthier during that time which gave me the opportunity to explore my interest in music. The Ace of Swords is meant to represent the actual condition of that time. It seems that my opinion of that stage of life was not too far off. It was a time of great learning and experiencing for me.

For the Father phase of my life, I chose the Eight of Stones which is the knowledge card. It represents the time of my life when I entered graduate school to earn my PhD. and then became a college professor. This, obviously, was a major experience for me. The interesting thing is that the card I pulled for that time of life was the Devil card. This card is meant to remind us that we should not take ourselves too seriously all the time. The Devil is the trickster. When we get too caught up in ourselves the Devil tells us to lighten up. I take this to mean that I should not get too pompous for my own good. I value the degrees I obtained but I must remember that they are not all that I am nor do they make me better or more deserving than anyone else. I obtained those degrees for myself and not to impress or demean anyone else.

As I enter the Sage phase of my life, I see myself more as a spiritual seeker than ever before. For that reason, I picked the Son of Cups to represent this time. The card I pulled for this stage, the Six of Wands, is the victory card. If I can focus my energy on this time of spiritual growth and renewal, I will be victorious.

Being Who You Are

6. Daily Readings
(a spread)

Many devoted Tarot users do a daily reading. Regular readings can provide some useful information about what the day may bring for you and it can be a way of bringing magick into everyday life. A reading can also be done in the evening to help provide insight or to provide a deeper reflection of the day's past events.

<u>Purpose</u>: To discover some information that would be useful for or about the day.

<u>Procedure</u>: Pull one card.

<u>Representations</u>:
1. If it is morning, pull a card that gives insight about the day to come, or
2. if it is evening, pull a card that reflects on the day just passed.

<u>Sample Reading:</u> 9 of Cups

This card is listed as the fortune card. It would appear that the day to come for me will be filled with good luck.

7. Affirmation
(a correspondence)

Sometimes you just need to believe in yourself and an affirmation can help you do that. You can either randomly pull a Major Arcana card and let the cards decide for you which affirmation you may need or you can select one from the list that is most appropriate for your situation. Repeat the affirmation often throughout the day and keep the card with you to remind you of it.

<u>Purpose</u>: To provide a positive statement for the day or whenever one is needed.

<u>Procedure:</u>

Pull or choose a Major Arcana card and relate it to the correspondence chart below.

1. Repeat that affirmation throughout the day or whenever it will be needed.

Table 2.1 Affirmation Correspondences

Card	Correspondence
0 The Fool	I will make a fresh start
I The Magician	I will transform myself
II The High Priestess	I will seek wisdom from within
III The Empress	I will be compassionate
IV The Emperor	I will create great things
V Hierophant	I will learn and grow
VI The Lovers	I am loved
VII Chariot	I will succeed
VIII Strength	I will be strong
IX The Hermit	I will consider my actions
X The Wheel of Fortune	I will not fear change
XI Justice	I will seek balance
XII The Hanged Man	I will celebrate my uniqueness
XIII Death	I will be reborn
XIV Alchemy	I will be in control
XV The Devil	I will overcome temptation
XVI The Tower	I will overcome adversity
XVII The Star	I will remain hopeful
XVIII The Moon	I will hold on to my dreams
XIX The Sun	I will celebrate life
XX Aeon	I will be patient

Card	Correspondence
XXI The Universe	I will encourage peace
0 The Multiverse	I will be free
blank card	I will not fear the mystery

8. Fulfilling Your Destiny
(a spread)

This spread will help provide more information to the activity you did earlier with numerology (activity number 3). In order to do this activity, you will first need to discover your numerology numbers and find the Major Arcana cards that correspond to those numbers. You could, of course, do this spread and randomly pull all the cards instead. After placing your destiny cards, the rest of the spread will help you determine how you can manifest your destiny in the coming day, month, and year. This is a spread that should not be done more than once a year.

Purpose: To learn how to fulfill the destiny revealed to you through numerology.

Preparation: Do activity number 3 and remove the Major Arcana cards used.

Procedure:
1. Place your Destiny Number card in the following spread.
2. Place your Day Number card in the following spread.
3. Place your Month Number card in the following spread.
4. Place your Year Number card in the following spread.
5. Pull three more cards and place in the following spread.

Drawing 5

Representations:
1. Your Destiny Number card
2. Your Day Number card
3. Your Month Number card
4. Your Year Number card
5. How to fulfill your destiny for the coming day
6. How to fulfill your destiny for the coming month
7. How to fulfill your destiny for the coming year

Sample Reading:
1. IV Emperor
2. 0 Fool
3. The Void
4. The Void
5. 6 of Wands
6. 5 of Stones
7. Father of Swords

From doing activity number 3, I discovered that my destiny card is the Emperor card and I took this card to mean that I need to bring forth something material and creative in my life which I am doing through my writing. My day card is the Fool and I need to manifest my destiny in the following day through the 6 of Wands. This is a card of great intellect so I take this to mean that I must spend the following day doing some research in my area of writing. My month card is the Void card and should be manifest in the coming month through the 5 of Stones. My material concerns may make it difficult for me to be creative during the next month. I will have to deal with those challenges before I will be able to continue. My year card, also the Void, will be manifested through the Father of Swords or Leadership card. I will need to take some leadership in bringing my writing forth.

9. Personal Qualities
(a discovery)

This is a simple activity but one which can help provide you with some interesting information. The more you meditate on the card you pull, the more you may learn. Choose a card from your deck and then compare how that card is similar or different from you. Allow your mind to free associate with all the imagery and symbolism in the card.

Purpose: To learn about yourself.

Procedure: Pull a card. Study the card and identify the things within the card that are similar to you and your personality and also identify those things that are different from you.

Sample Reading: 4 of Wands

The 4 of Wands in my deck is subtitled "perfection.". I know I am certainly not perfect but the card does seem to indicate that perfection is sought through balance and I constantly strive for balance in my life. Through the elements, I work very hard to make sure that I pay attention to the needs of my body, mind, heart, and soul while also keeping my attention on the call to Spirit.

10. Solving Problems
(a correspondence)

There are always those times when you just do not know what to do and it helps to have something aid you in making a decision. In those times, the Tarot can help. This is a sample procedure for finding a quick answer or inspiration for taking the next step.

Purpose: To find a quick solution to a problem.

Procedure:
1. Concentrate upon your situation.
2. Pull a Major Arcana card and refer to the correspondence chart.

Table 2.2 Solutions Correspondence

Card	Correspondence
0 The Fool	go forth
I The Magician	learn more
II The High Priestess	pray or meditate upon it
III The Empress	be compassionate
IV The Emperor	define boundaries
V Hierophant	teach or instruct
VI The Lovers	see the overall picture
VII Chariot	find a clear path
VIII Strength	seek balance
IX The Hermit	withdraw
X The Wheel of Fortune	look for a change
XI Justice	be forthright and take action
XII The Hanged Man	see a new viewpoint
XIII Death	find the truth

Card	Correspondence
XIV Alchemy	restrain yourself
XV The Devil	laugh it off
XVI The Tower	destroy falsity
XVII The Star	Be creative and hopeful
XVIII The Moon	follow your heart
XIX The Sun	seek growth and the positive
XX Aeon	find mediation
XXI The Universe	unite
0 The Multiverse	seek the ultimate reality
blank card	Do nothing until the answer is revealed

Chapter 3

The Moon and Magick

Introduction

he moon is the "planet" that symbolizes magick and dreams. We see it best at night when the sun has gone away. In the mystery of the dark we wrestle with our fears and attempt to control our environment so that we can sleep peacefully and dream pleasant thoughts. One way that people used to try and control the world around them was through magick. The appearance of the moon calls us to do magick and ritual and to understand our dreams and hopes. An important part of any ritual is develop the ability to meditate. This chapter will include activities to aid in meditation.

Magick

11. Magick For Yourself
(a spread)

If you find yourself doing the same old ritual every day week then use this simple spread to help you understand what you need to focus upon in your next personal ritual. This spread will describe to you what it is you need to bring into your life in order to keep your life full of magick and it will describe how you can do that through ritual.

Purpose: To determine what you may need for a particular ritual.

Procedure: Pull two cards and place in the following spread.

Drawing 6

Representations:
1. What you need to bring into your life.
2. How to bring that into your life through ritual.

Sample Reading:
1. XVIII The Moon
2. Son of Cups

What I need to bring into my life is something that may be revealed to me through my dreams (The Moon) and the way to do that is through consciously seeking it (Son of Cups). I need to do a ritual that will help me connect to my dreams.

12. Magick For Others
(a spread)

In the last spread, you found out what magick you needed to do for yourself. Here, you can find out how to help others through your rituals. Pull cards to determine who needs help and how you can offer that help through a ritual. Remember to only offer positive energy. It is best to always ask permission before sending energy to another person but if you cannot, then make sure that energy is as pure and positive as possible. Remember that all good rituals should be followed by concrete action as well.

Purpose: To determine what you can do through ritual to help someone else.

Procedure: Pull three cards.

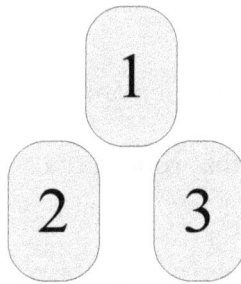

```
        ┌─────┐
        │  1  │
        └─────┘
   ┌─────┐ ┌─────┐
   │  2  │ │  3  │
   └─────┘ └─────┘
```

Drawing 7

Representations:
1. Who may need help.
2. What help is needed.
3. How to help.

Sample Reading:
1. 5 of Cups
2. 4 of Wands
3. Mother of Wands

The first card (5 of Cups) indicates that I must think of someone I know who has encountered a recent disappointment in life. I know of someone who has recently lost his job so I will focus upon him for my ritual. What he needs is a sense of emotional balance (4 of Wands) which I can help him get through sending feelings of compassion (Mother of Wands). I need to do a ritual to send compassion and feelings of acceptance to him. I also need to give him a call.

13. The Tarot Card Talisman
(a correspondence)

Tarot cards can make excellent talismans. A talisman is an object you use to infuse with energy or to represent a magickal goal or need. In either one of the two previous spreads in which you did a ritual, you could use a card to represent that goal then carry that card with you throughout the day as a talisman to remind you of your goal. Talismans are a good way to keep your focus upon your objective throughout the day.

Purpose: To use a tarot card as a magickal talisman.

Procedure: Choose a card that represents a particular goal or need you have.

14. Mysterious Manifestation
(a spread)

Here's a way to put a little fun and mystery into your rituals. With this spread you will work to manifest a magickal goal which will be unknown to you. The cards will tell you how to bring that mysterious goal into your life and how you will know when it has been done. You will want only positive things to be manifest so if you do not believe all your cards have positive aspects then remove any negative cards from the deck before beginning.

Purpose: To bring a mysterious but positive event or manifestation into your life.

Procedure:
1. Pull a card.
2. Pull a second card without looking at it and place it face down.
3. Pull a third card.

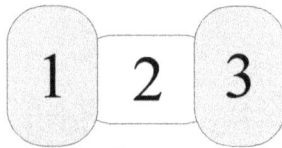

Drawing 8

Representations:
1. How to manifest the mystery.
2. The mysterious goal.
3. How you will know when the magick has taken place.

Sample Reading:
1. I The Magician
2. ???
3. 9 of Cups

In order to manifest the mystery of card no 2, I will need to enact a ritual (The Magician) asking that it be manifest for good and right. The 9 of Cups tells me that when I receive a gift of any small fortune that I will know that the mystery has been brought forth. After that point I can look at the second card and see what it was that was meant for me.

Dreamwork

15. Dream Interpretation
(a discovery)

This discovery is an easy way to get more insight to your mysterious dreams. Match images from your dreams to images in the cards. If you have several decks, use them all to find as many images as possible. Let the cards provide you with further insight into your dreams.

Purpose: To discover more information about dreams.

Procedure:
1. Write down a recent dream and note as many images as you can remember.
2. Find tarot cards that have similar images.
3. Use the information provided by the tarot cards to provide additional information about your dreams.

16. Desired Dreams
(a correspondence)

Let the cards provide you the magick you need to create your own desired dreams. Put together a dream sequence using the cards and then place them under your pillow in the order you want them to be seen. Do a short ritual to bring forth the dreams you desire, drink some dream inducing tea, and then prepare for a magickal evening. You could also use this method to encourage prophetic dreams about particular people or events.

Purpose: To encourage particular dreams during sleep.

Procedure:
1. Choose cards that have images you wish to envision during your dreams.
2. Place the cards in a desired order under your pillow before you sleep.

Meditation

17. The Zen Koan
(a spread)

A *koan* is a special technique in Zen Buddhism used to reach enlightenment. The idea is that a Zen student works through a seemingly impossible question with his or her teacher until an answer can be found which brings the student closer to understanding universal truth. One of the most famous koans is the question: what is the sound of one hand clapping? With the Tarot you can create your own Zen koan and then seek a mystical answer.

Purpose: To discover great wisdom through the creation of a Tarot koan.

Procedure:
1. Pull a number card to represent the type of question according to the following table.

Table 3.1 Question Correspondence

Card	Question
Ace	why
Two	what
Three	when
Four	where
Five	who
Six	how
Six	which
Seven	could
Eight	should
Nine	does

2. Pull two more cards.
3. Pull a final card and lay it face down until ready.

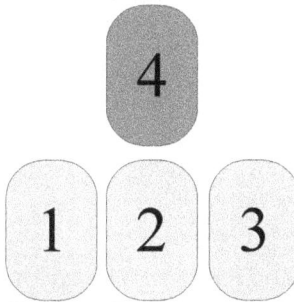

Drawing 9

Representations:
   1. The beginning of the question.
   2. The object of the question.
   3. The focus of the question.
   4. Insight into the answer.

Sample Reading:
   1. Ace of Cups

2. V Hierophant
3. Father of Wands
4. Ace of Stones

First, I had to form the question which I read as: why (Ace of Cups) does learning (Hierophant) lead to emotional maturity (Father of Wands)? I left the fourth card face down until I finished contemplating the question. The answer I came up with is that learning helps me understand the world and, thus, helps me to feel more secure about who I am and what my place in the universe may be. This, in turn, gives me emotional strength. My answer was confirmed by the Ace of Stones I turned over since the Ace represents abundance.

18. Tarot Mandala
(a discovery)

A *mandala* is a complex image used for meditation. Its purpose is to draw you into the center of the design so that you are pulled into your own center where you can meditate deeply. In this activity, you will use the cards to create a mandala upon which you can meditate. This is one of the few activities that uses the back of the cards as well as the front. Begin by taking out all the Aces from the deck.

Purpose: To use the cards to create a mandala for meditating upon.

Procedure:
1. Pull a card to be the focus of the meditation.
2. Place the remaining cards in the following way.
3. Begin with following formation then add cards around it to create as large a mandala as you desire. Be creative with your design.

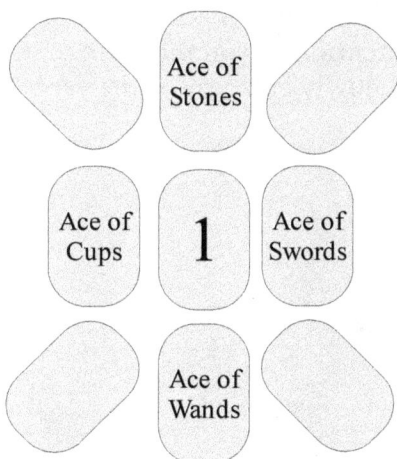

Drawing 10

19. Tarot Scrying
(a discovery)

Similar to the above activity, the Tarot cards can also be used to scry. *Scrying* involves meditating upon a dark or translucent object in order to allow images or messages to reach you from your subconscious. Common items used for scrying are dark mirrors, dark bowls of water, and crystal balls. To scry, look intensely into the object and clear your mind. Slowly allow images to form within the object that you can interpret later. To do this activity you should have a dark surface like a table with a black cloth over it. Sometimes a reflective surface helps so a black table with a glass top could also be very useful. With the Tarot, however, you can add an extra step to your scrying by encouraging images to come to the center. In this formation, you will place two cards on either side of the meditation space to inform the scrying process.

Purpose: To encourage a scrying meditation through the cards.

Procedure:
1. Clear a black or dark space upon your table.
2. Place the backs of the cards around the space in the following formation.

3. Place two cards face up on either side of the formation.
4. Focus your attention as you meditate on the center. Let the two outside cards slowly enter the center and begin to form images.

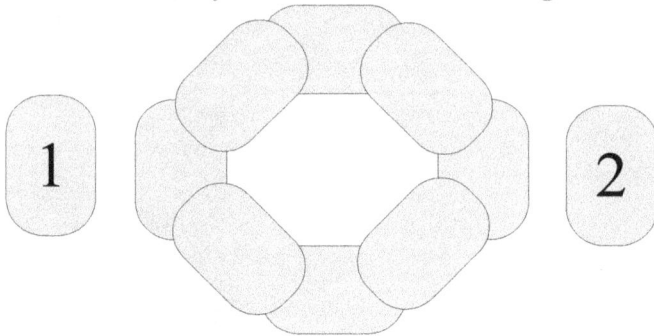

Drawing 11

20. Tarot Yoga
(a correspondence)

Tarot cards can be helpful in beginning or providing variety to a Yoga or other exercise program. Choose your favorite postures and assign them to the cards or use the correspondence in the appendix of this book. Use the cards to pick a posture for the day or to choose several positions. Place the cards in an order and create a movement pattern such as one might do for Tai Chi. Chi King and Tai Chi postures can also be done in this manner.

Purpose: To help choose a variety of postures through the cards.

Procedure: Assign postures to the cards then choose as many cards for each posture needed.

Chapter 4

Mercury and the Mind

Introduction

Mercury is the winged god and messenger to the gods. He helps the gods communicate. The planet Mercury, then, represents forms of communication as well as the mind - for the mind is the originator of all our messages. This chapter will include activities to help you improve the mind through learning and help you work to communicate with others and the gods.

Learning

21. Which Subject?
(a correspondence)

There are hundreds of subjects that any one person can begin to study and some people spend their entire lives studying only one thing. Others, though, may want to learn a little about a lot of things. We tend to view the world in categories and divisions but I believe that the more you learn, the more you discover that all knowledge eventually merges. Studied deeply enough all subjects of interest share similarities. With this activity, the cards will help you choose a subject of study upon which you can increase your knowledge and understanding of the world.

Purpose: To determine a subject of study.

Procedure:

1. Create a correspondence chart related to subjects of study or use the one included here.
2. Separate your Minor Arcana cards out from the rest of the deck.
3. Pull one Minor Arcana card to determine the general subject category.
4. D) Pull one Minor Arcana card to determine the specific subject category.
5. E) Once you have identified a specific category, go to a library or bookstore and browse that section until you find a book that interests you.

Table 4.1 General Subject Category Correspondences

Card	General Subject
Ace	Philosophy and Psychology
Two	Religion
Three	Social Sciences
Four	Language
Five	Natural Science/ Math
Six	Applied Sciences
Seven	The Arts
Eight	Literature
Nine	Geography
Ten	History

Table 4.2 Specific Subject Correspondences 1 - 5

Card	Philosophy/ Psychology	Religion	Social Sciences	Language	Natural science/ Math
Ace	particular philosophies	Christianity	Sociology	Language research	algebra
2	metaphysics	Judaism	anthropology	Language theory	geometry
3	cosmology	Islam	statistics	linguistics	calculus

Card	Philosophy/ Psychology	Religion	Social Sciences	Language	Natural science/ Math
4	epistemology	Buddhism	Political science	Writing systems	astronomy
5	the occult	Taoism	economics	etymology	Earth sciences
6	applied psychology	Hinduism	law	English grammar	physics
7	logic and reasoning	Other religions	government	Western languages	chemistry
8	ethics	Religious texts	Social services	Other languages	anthropology
9	ancient philosophies	Religious history	education	Ancient Western	biology
10	modern philosophies	comparative	culture	Other ancient	botany

Table 4.3 Specific Subject Correspondence Table 6 - 10

No.	Applied Sciences	The Arts	Literature	Geography	History
Ace	Traditional medicine	architecture	American literature	U.S. Geography	American history
2	Experimental medicine	sculpture	English literature	N. American Geography	European history
3	anatomy	drawing	European literature	European Geography	Modern world history
4	Family living	painting	World literature	African Geography	Ancient world history
5	engineering	Graphic arts	Ancient literature	Asian Geography	travel
6	agriculture	photography	poetry	Other world geography	Ancient history
7	economics	music	fiction	Extra-terrestial geography	biography
8	Business management	dance	Non-fiction	Map making	Natural history

No.	Applied Sciences	The Arts	Literature	Geography	History
9	chemistry	film	drama	American travel	genealogy
10	manufacturing	Sports and games	speech	World travel	Extra-terrestial history

22. Which Book?
(a correspondence)

There are thousands of books out there for you to read. You want to learn but you do not know which book you should read. Many of the world's books are listed in the Library of Congress Catalog which is available on-line. In this activity, you will search the LC catalog on-line to find a book to read. However, you should know that you may be directed to some very obscure books that may not be of any interest to you. If that is the case, you can re-do the activity to find another book or you can allow the book you do find spark your imagination for reading something else. The Library of Congress catalogs its books through a system of one or two letters followed by a set of numbers. To find a book, go to the Library of Congress website: http://catalog.loc.gov. Go to <Basic Search>. Under "Search" click <Call Number Browse>. Select 25 records per page. In "Search Text" type in your call number and you will be given the first 25 entries that appear with that call number or its closest equivalent. In this activity, you will find two letters and four numbers. You will need to separate your Major Arcana cards from the Minor arcana and Court cards.

Purpose: To find a book to read.

Procedure:
1. Pull a Major Arcana card and relate it to the letter correspondence chart.
2. Pull a second Major Arcana card to get a second letter.
3. Pull a card from the Minor Arcana and Court cards to get a

number.

(Court cards = 0, 10 = 0)

4. Pull a second number card.
5. Pull a third number card.
6. Pull a fourth number card.
7. Pull a third Major Arcana card to choose the exact book.

Table 4.4 Letter Correspondences

Card	Correspondence
0 The Fool	A
I The Magician	B
II The High Priestess	G, Gh
III The Empress	D, Dh
IV The Emperor	H
V Hierophant	O
VI The Lovers	E
VII Chariot	C, Ch
VIII Strength	F
IX The Hermit	I, Y
X The Wheel of Fortune	K, Kh
XI Justice	L
XII The Hanged Man	M
XIII Death	N
XIV Alchemy	S
XV The Devil	H
XVI The Tower	P, Ph
XVII The Star	J
XVIII The Moon	Q,U
XIX The Sun	R
XX Aeon	S, Sh

Card	Correspondence
XXI The Universe	`T, Th
0 The Multiverse	
blank card	the void

Table 4.5 Library of Congress Cataloging Letters

Call Letter	Subject
B	Philosophy, Psychology, Religion
C	Auxiliary Sciences of History
D	History: General and Europe
E	History: America
F	History: America
A	General Works
G	Geography, Anthropology, Recreation
H	Social Sciences
J	Political Science
K	Law
L	Education
M	Music
N	Fine Arts
P	Language and Literature
Q	Science
R	Medicine
S	Agriculture
T	Technology
U	Military Science
V	Naval Science
Z	Bibliography, Library Science

<u>Sample Reading:</u>
1. XII The Hanged Man (=M)
2. 0 The Multiverse (=V,W)
3. 6 of Cups
4. 9 of Wands
5. 9 of Swords
6. 9 of Cups
7. XV The Devil

The Catalog classification I looked up was MV 6999 which I typed into the LC website search engine and clicked "call number browse." I was given 25 choices. I looked at the 15th entry and was led to a sound recording titled Zinga. I then looked at an on-line music source for Zinga and found a group called Zingaia. I doubt it was the same thing as the listing in the LC catalog but I found some interesting music that I might never have discovered before.

23. Which Passage?
(a discovery)

In this activity, you will be asked to read sections from some of your favorite books to remind you of your insights and learnings from that book. First, you will need to identify 24 books that you own or can easily get your hands on; they should be books of wisdom and inspiration for you. Make a correspondence list with those books. Then, you will use the cards to determine the page from which you will get your quotation or section to read. You will need to pull all three cards at once in a particular order so you may have to shuffle and pull cards several times to get the right combination.

<u>Purpose</u>: To obtain a random passage from a book from which you can reflect and gain inspiration.

<u>Procedure</u>:
1. Shuffle and pull three cards until you get the following combination:
   a) A Major Arcana card that determines which book to use.
   b) A Minor Arcana or Court card that determines the page

number in the tens.
(Court cards =0)
   c) A Minor Arcana or Court card to determine the page number in the ones.

2. If you do not get this combination, then shuffle and pull three cards again.
3. Note how many times is takes you to get the right combination. Go to the book and page number indicated. The number of times it took you to get the correct combination can determine the paragraph or sentence from which you should read.
4. Go to that section and read the passage. Contemplate or meditate upon it.

<u>Sample Reading</u>:
   1. The Universe
   2. Ace of Wands
   3. 2 of Swords

I am to choose a quotation from the 21st book on my list (The Universe). I assigned the Tao Te Ching as my 21st book. After six shuffles, I finally get the right combination. From the Ace of Wands I get the number one and the 2 of Swords gives me a 2. I turn to page 21 of the book. Instead of page numbers, I chose to use the numbers assigned to the individual sayings of the book so I turned to number 21 and went to the sixth sentence which reads: "Those essences the truth enfold of what, when seen, shall then be told." It certainly is an obscure sentence and will give me much to reflect upon.

24. Discovering Truth
(a discovery)

Similar to the Zen Koan activity, this activity leads to the creation of a sentence that can reveal an interesting insight upon which you can ponder. In this case, the cards relate to parts of a sentence. Use your creative powers to provide the type of words into the sentence that would help to create a complete sentence.

<u>Purpose</u>: To create a sentence that contains a deep truth.

<u>Procedure</u>: (4 cards)
1. Start the sentence with "The," "A," or "An."
2. Pull a card and create from it a noun.
3. Pull a card and create from it a verb.
4. Pull a card and create from it another noun.
5. Add a preposition or connection word.
6. Add another "The," "A," or "An."
7. Pull a card and create from it another noun.

Use the cards to complete a sentence that would look something like:

The/A/An _____ _____ _____ [   ] the/a/an _____
            noun   verb   noun   preposition   noun

<u>Sample Reading</u>:
1. The Hanged Man
2. 6 of Swords
3. Death
4. Father of Cups

    From these cards I derived the sentence: the unique (Hanged Man as noun) learn (6 of Swords as verb) renewal (Death as noun) through (preposition) the guiding of others (Father of Cups as noun). This created a rather profound statement. Those who are willing to escape the constant demands of the personal ego are unique people. They see the world differently and learn that we are here to help one another. Doing this not only aids others, it leads to renewal of the person doing the helping. The Death card is about major renewal - not just small changes. When one can guide another person as a parent guides a child to grow and develop, great learning takes place to the person receiving the care and attention but, even more significantly, the person providing the guidance is also enriched.

25. The Tarot Scavenger Hunt
(a discovery)

This activity could be a lot of fun for yourself and a group of others. The cards create for you a list of things to find as in a scavenger hunt. You would first determine what the cards call you to find and then you would have to search for those things in your surroundings. With each find, take careful note to observe what you should learn from seeking this object and finding it where it is. In other words, you are seeking out truth from the search for common or unusual objects. With a group of people, you could create the list together and then have a race to see who is the first to collect the objects. That person would also reveal the truths he or she learned along the way. You could use as many cards as you like to create your list but we will use only three here as an example.

Purpose: To create a list of common or unusual objects for you to find and then learn from the process of seeking them out.

Procedure: (3 cards)
1.   Pull a card to determine the first object to seek.
2.   Pull a card to determine the second object to seek.
3.   Pull a card to determine the third object to seek.

Sample Reading:
1.   10 of Stones
2.   The Lovers
3.   6 of Stones

I would need to find the following objects in order: a lost coin (10 of Stones), a pair of lovers (The Lovers), and a butterfly (an image on the 6 of Stones) and then notice the circumstances in which I am in when I find these things so that I can learn from them.

Communicating

26. Tarot Gematria
(a discovery)

In the practice of *gematria*, letters in words are given number equivalents. From the numerical representations of those numbers, it is believed that deeper meanings of the words can be discovered. Words with similar numbers are also considered to be significant. For example, many people know the significance of the number 666 in the last book of the Bible. It is considered by some to be an evil number. One reason this number is believed to be significant is because when the Emperor Nero's original Greek name is changed into numbers it becomes 666. Nero was not a particularly nice guy to the Jews so one can understood why he might be called the evil beast. Of course, his name could not be stated outright so a number code was assigned to it. By finding a number and a Tarot card equivalent to a word or phrase, you can gain a deeper insight into that word or phrase. As in the numerology activity, you will first need to find a number less than 25 which is equivalent to the words you are studying and then compare that number to the related Major Arcana card.

<u>Purpose</u>: To discover deeper meanings of words and phrases through the Tarot.

<u>Procedure</u>:
1. Select a word or phrase to study.
2. Reduce the words to a number less than 25 using the chart below.
3. Compare that number to the equivalent Major Arcana card.

Table 4.6 Letters to Numbers

1	2	3	4	5	6	7	8	9
A	B	C	D	E	F	G	H	I
J	K	L	M	N	O	P	Q	R
S	T	U	V	W	X	Y	Z	

<u>Sample Reading</u>:

I chose the word "happiness" and determined the following numbers:
h = 8, a = 1, p = 7, p = 7, i = 9, n = 5, e = 5, s = 1, s = 1
8+1+7+7+9+5+5+1+1 = 44
4+4 = 8
The VIII card is Strength. From this I read that it takes courage and strength in your convictions and a belief in yourself to be happy.

27. Writing a Tarot Code
(a correspondence)

The Tarot can be used to create a coded message to others who understand the Tarot and the code pattern you are using. You can create a simple substitution code by changing letters with Tarot numbers or symbols. For the first method, change the letters of each word with the numbers of the Major Arcana card related to that letter from the letter correspondence chart. For the second method, change letters according to the letter and Major Arcana symbol chart included below.

<u>Purpose</u>: To create a coded message using the Tarot.

<u>Procedure</u>:
1. Choose a word or phrase to encode.
2. Change the letters in the word or phrase according to one of two substitution systems.

System One:
1. change letters according to the related Tarot card number.
2. use the roman numeral and separate with dots
3. use an asterisk for the Multiverse card and parentheses for the blank card
4. put a 2 or other number in front of repeated letters
5. use a dash to separate words

System Two:
1. change letters according to the related Tarot card and symbol.
2. use a another symbol as a separator
3. use another symbol such as an "X" before doubled letters

Table 4.7 Symbol Correspondence

Card	Letter	Symbol	
0 The Fool	A	s	question mark
I The Magician	B	e	athame
II The High Priestess	G, Gh	g	chalice
III The Empress	D, Dh	J	female
IV The Emperor	H	K	male
V Hierophant	O	a	check mark
VI The Lovers	E	Y	heart
VII Chariot	C, Ch	l	compass
VIII Strength	F	+	lightning
IX The Hermit	I, Y	¢	mirror
X The Wheel of Fortune	K, Kh	Z	wheel
XI Justice	L	=	dove
XII The Hanged Man	M	m	man
XIII Death	N	N	skull
XIV Alchemy	S	i	cauldron
XV The Devil	H	o	horns
XVI The Tower	P, Ph	G	building
XVII The Star	J	r	star
XVIII The Moon	Q, U	N	moon
XIX The Sun	R	a	sun
XX Aeon	S, Sh	y	egg

Card	Letter	Symbol	
XXI The Universe	T, Th	1	number 1
0 The Multiverse	V, W	q	infinity symbol
blank card	XZ	◯	0
separator		n	dot

<u>Sample Reading</u>:

I can encode the phrase "happiness for all" one of two ways. In the first the word is changed into numbers to get IV.0.2XVI.IX.XIII.VI.2XX-VIII.V.XIX-0.2XI.

The second method changes the phrase into symbols to get:
K **?** 🏛2▦♟♥y2●🦡✔a●**?**=2

28. Communicating With Other Life
(a spread)

Have you ever wanted to know just exactly what your favorite pet is thinking? There are many good sources that can teach you how to practice animal communication but I have found that the ability needed to do that varies with different people. For those who do not seem to possess the natural talent to understand the language of other creatures, this activity may help. It requires that you enter a deep meditative space with another animal who is willing to share their thoughts with you.

<u>Purpose</u>: To communicate with another non-human being.

<u>Procedure</u>:
1. Enter into a meditative state in the presence of the animal.
2. Ask permission to communicate with that being.
3. Ask a question or ask that you experience the thoughts of the animal.
4. Clear your mind and concentrate on you and it being of one mind.
5. Allow the creature to tell you how many cards to pull.

6. Pull that number of cards and discern your answer.

29. The Right Question
(a spread)

When seeking advice or information, identifying the right question can be as important as finding an answer. In this exercise, you will form a question that can then be asked as you would in a standard Tarot divination.

<u>Purpose</u>: To find a question to be used for divination.

<u>Procedure</u>:
1. Pull a Minor Arcana card to get a question word.
2. Pull two more cards.
3. Formulate a question.

<u>Representations</u>:
1. Question word.
2. Subject word.
3. Object word.

Table 4.8 Question Correspondence

Card	Question
Ace	why is/are
Two	what is/are
Three	when is/are
Four	where is/are
Five	who is/are
Six	how is/are
Seven	which is/are
Eight	could/ should I
Nine	do/ does

<u>Sample Reading</u>:
1. 10 of Swords
2. VI The Lovers
3. 7 of Stones

The question I formed is: Do (10 of Swords) lovers (The Lovers) become useless (7 of Stones)? It seems like a rather depressing question and not one I might have normally asked in a divination session but I decided to pursue it anyway. To answer the question you could use any number of standard Tarot spreads. I decided to use a simple one card spread and pulled another card which was the Father of Wands. In my deck, this card represents intelligence so I took my answer to be that all relationships become useless when there is no consistent thought behind keeping them alive and meaningful. Without constant care, a plant can wither away and die. The same is true for all relationships; they need care, feeding, and attention and this comes in the form of how you think about your lover and the relationship itself.

30. Sending A Message
(a spread)

I know I do not always keep up with my communication with others as much as I should. With this activity you can find out who it is you should contact and how. You will need to let your imagination search for an interpretation of what the cards are trying to tell you.

<u>Purpose</u>: To determine who you should contact with a particular message.

<u>Procedure</u>:
1. Pull three cards and lay out in order.
2. Determine the message that is needed to be sent.
3. Send the message.

<u>Representations</u>:
1. The message to be delivered.
2. To whom the message should be delivered.

3. How the message should be delivered.

Sample Reading:
1. 8 of Cups
2. Son of Wands
3. 9 of Wands

I determined that I needed to express my failure at something (8 of Cups) to a young emotional male (Son of Wands) through a high energy method (9 of Wands). From this, I decided that I had failed to express my feelings to some of my friends about recent events and that I needed to reach out to them. I decided to write an e-mail to a friend of mine who has been very supportive of me but who I had not thanked often enough.

Chapter 5

Venus and Relationships

Introduction

enus is the famous goddess of beauty and love. She is one of the most well known goddesses because her name was called upon so frequently. We all want to have positive, strong, and nurturing relationships and Venus is the one to seek for helping with these things. After all, love is how we come close to the source of all life. We seek the beautiful through nature and through art. In this chapter, we will look at how to develop and strengthen relationships and how to be creative through the Tarot.

Relationships

31. Finding Love
(a spread)

I cannot tell you how many times, when I was reading Tarot cards professionally, that people would come to me to seek their soul-mate. We all seek that perfect partner. I always tell people that there is no such thing as the absolutely perfect lover. All relationships take work but it is certainly true that some partnerships are easier than others. In this activity, you will be given some information on to how you can find a special someone. This spread is geared toward finding a love relationship but it could easily be adapted for other partnerships as well.

In order to find someone, you have to be willing to go out and meet him or her and be willing to talk and engage that person. If you sit at home all day you can be assured that you will never meet anyone at all.

<u>Purpose</u>: To help find a special person.

<u>Procedure</u>: Pull five cards in the pattern below.

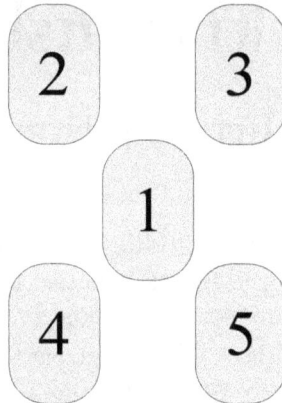

Drawing 12

<u>Representations</u>:
1. A clue as to who the person is.
2. Where you should go to meet this person.
3. What you should be doing.
4. How you should approach the person.
5. How to know if you have found the right person.

<u>Sample Reading</u>:
1. V The Emperor
2. Daughter of Cups
3. II The High Priestess
4. XVI The Tower
5. 6 of Wands

Since I am happily married I did not need to do this spread to find a romantic partner. Instead, I did a hypothetical spread in which I imagined a young woman who had come to me seeking a romantic relationship for herself. The spread told me that she would meet a fairly typical male friend who might be a bit on the conservative side (The Emperor) and that she would meet him at a social gathering of young spiritually minded people (Daughter of Cups). In order to meet him, she would need to be discussing spiritual matters or meditating (The High Priestess). She should approach him boldly and without concern of how others might view her (The Tower). She would know him by his intelligent conversation of things which he felt passionately about (6 of Wands).

32. Understanding A Relationship
(a spread)

All relationships take some degree of work to keep them healthy and alive. We all grow and change and sometimes people are not able to grow together or they learn to support each other through that growth. Inevitably, all relationships will have their ups and downs. In the more challenging times it helps to be able to understand what is needed in the relationship in order to encourage growth and forward movement. This spread can help you gain some information on how to help a struggling relationship.

Purpose: To find out how to promote growth in a relationship.

Procedure:
1. Choose a card to represent yourself in the relationship.
2. Choose a card that represents what you want in the relationship.
3. Pull three more cards and place in the following spread.

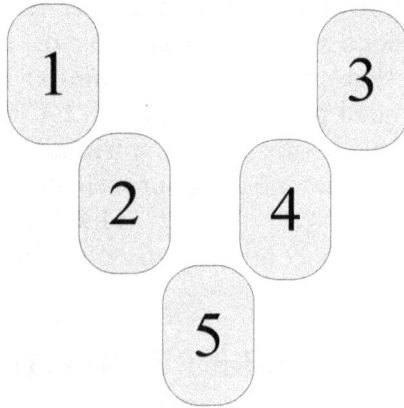

Drawing 13

Representations:
1. Yourself.
2. What you want from the relationship.
3. The other person.
4. What that person wants from the relationship.
5. How to bring together both desires in order to promote growth.

Sample Reading:
1. 2 of Wands
2. XVII The Star
3. VI The Lovers
4. 10 of Wands
5. 2 of Cups

Once again I will do a hypothetical reading. In this spread, the person doing the reading is one who has experienced great emotional change in the relationship (2 of Wands) but remains hopeful that these changes will not damage the couple's feelings for each other (The Star). The other person in this pairing is deeply in love with the first (The Lovers) but is feeling somewhat caged-in lately and desires some sense of freedom (10 of Wands). The solution to their dilemma is to focus on their love for each other and allow this sense of change to take its natural course. Fear of change will separate them but strength and belief in the relationship will keep them together (2 of Cups).

33. Maintaining Relationships
(a spread)

This activity assumes that you are in a fairly positive relationship but seek to know what you can do to maintain the strength of that experience.

<u>Purpose</u>: To find out what you can do to maintain a good relationship.

<u>Procedure</u>:
1. Choose a card to represent yourself.
2. Choose a card to represent the other person.
3. Pull two more cards and lay out in the following spread.

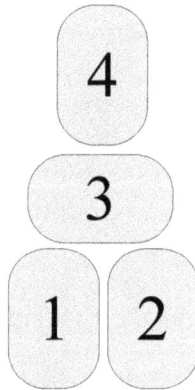

Drawing 14

<u>Representations</u>:
1. Yourself
2. The other person
3. Something that bonds the two of you together
4. What you can do to strengthen that bond.

<u>Sample Reading</u>:
1. Son of Cups
2. Ace of Wands
3. 2 of Stones
4. 5 of Cups

In this reading, I chose the Son of Cups to represent myself because I am always seeking answers while I chose the Ace of Wands to represent my partner who is creative and passionate. What holds us together is our sense of harmony - the way that we balance each other (2 of Stones). What can strengthen that harmony is the need to always support each other through our times of disappointment (5 of Cups).

34. Issues and Compatibility
(a spread)

All relationships involve some degree of conflict. If those times of disagreement can be seen as part of a natural growing process and if both sides of the disagreement can be open to hearing and accepting the views of the other side, then continued growth in the relationship can take place. Sometimes it helps to know how the other person in a conflict views the situation. At other times when there is no conflict, it can still be helpful to know how compatible two people may be together. In this activity, you will learn how to gain information about an issue in a relationship or about how compatible you may be with another person.

Purpose: To better understand the two sides of a disagreement.

Procedure:
1. Pull 10 cards and lay out in this order:

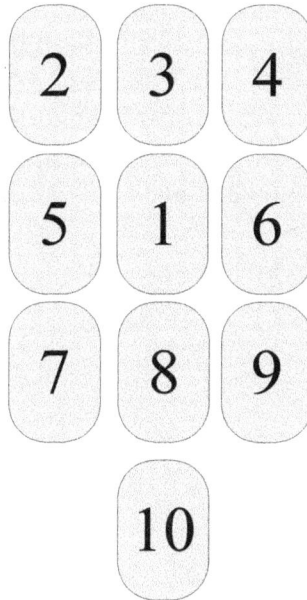

Drawing 15

2. Pull a number of cards until you come to a Minor Arcana card.
3. Stack the cards and place them in the position above according to the Minor Arcana card.
4. Pull a number of cards again until you come to another Minor Arcana card.
5. Stack the cards and place them in the position above according to the Minor Arcana card.

Representations:

There should be two stacks of cards in the positions described on the square chart. The locations of these stacks represent how the two of you will view each other either overall or in a particular situation. The square gives a graphic representation of compatibility. The two stacks are located according to the two Minor Arcana cards found.

1. Stacks on the same position = total agreement
2. Stacks on the same line = agreement (the closer the better)
3. Stacks on different lines = dissimilar viewpoints
4. Stacks on opposite lines = opposing viewpoints

5. A stack in the middle (1) can see all viewpoints
6. A stack on the outside (10) has difficulty seeing any other viewpoints.
7. Cards in the stacks depict factors influencing the person's viewpoint.
8. Cards in the square that intersect between the stacks can reveal how to
9. resolve differences.

<u>Sample Reading</u>:
1. 10 of Swords
2. 5 of Swords
3. 6 of Swords
4. Mother of Stones
5. 8 of Stones
6. 3 of Stones
7. 4 of Wands
8. 9 of Stones
9. Mother of Cups
10. 1VI The Lovers
11. myself) The High Priestess, Father of Wands, Ace of Cups
12. the other person) 2 of Swords

After pulling the 10 cards to give me the square, I pulled two cards until I got the Ace of Cups for myself and immediately pulled the 2 of Swords for the other person. I put the cards in the following order.

5 of Swords	6 of Swords	Mother of Stones
8 of Stones	10 of Swords	3 of Stones
4 of Wands	9 of Stones	Mother of Cups
	The Lovers	

I placed the stack of cards representing me atop the 10 of Swords (Ace of Cups) and placed the other stack atop the 5 of Swords (2 of Swords) which then gave me the revised spread. Note that underneath the Ace of Cups is the Father of Wands and the High

Priestess.

2 of Swords	6 of Swords	Mother of Stones
8 of Stones	Ace of Cups*	3 of Stones
4 of Wands	9 of Stones	Mother of Cups
	The Lovers	

It would appear that because my stack is in the middle of the square that I will be able to find common ground better than the other person. The other person will eventually be able to see my point of view though I am not sure how since no other cards came to appear in his stack. I will have to be the patient one and the peacemaker on the road to resolution and I will have to use careful thought (Father of Wands) with a focus on spiritual enlightenment and meditation (The High Priestess) to encourage understanding between us.

35. Finding A Familiar
(a correspondence)

A *familiar* is an animal companion but, more than that, a familiar is a connection to another being who can aid you in doing magick and in relating to Spirit. A familiar can be a real animal like a house pet or it can be a creature from another realm. There are several decks such as the Animal Wise Tarot, the Australian Animal Tarot, the Druid Animal Oracle, and the Medicine Cards which feature animals but it is not necessary that you buy a special deck just for this purpose. In this activity, the Tarot will help you identify what kind of animal you should seek for your familiar.

Purpose: To seek your animal familiar

Procedure:
   1.   Pull a Major Arcana card and relate it to the correspondence

chart.

2. Meditate and seek out the animal selected.

Table 5.1 Animal Correspondence

Card	Correspondence
0 The Fool	Hummingbird
I The Magician	Raven
II The High Priestess	Raccoon
III The Empress	Cat
IV The Emperor	Dog
V Hierophant	Lion
VI The Lovers	Otter
VII Chariot	Horse
VIII Strength	Bear
IX The Hermit	Skunk
X The Wheel of Fortune	Frog
XI Justice	Dove
XII The Hanged Man	Bat
XIII Death	Snake
XIV Alchemy	Squirrel
XV The Devil	Coyote
XVI The Tower	Fox
XVII The Star	Firefly
XVIII The Moon	Dragonfly
XIX The Sun	Rabbit
XX Aeon	Butterfly
XXI The Universe	Spider
0 The Multiverse	Hawk
blank card	Owl

The Arts

36. Writing Music
(a discovery)

It is possible to use operations of chance to compose music. John Cage was a modern composer that spent much of his life exploring just this idea. Though it is an intriguing idea to write a piece of music all from chance operations, the result tends to be devoid of the warmth and beauty of the human touch. Sometimes, though, using chance can help a composer explore possibilities for new ideas. In this case, the Tarot can offer some ways to try out new musical ideas. To do this, you will use the planetary heptagram with the Major Arcana to find notes within a particular scale. Chromatics can be added through the use of the Minor Arcana and additional symbols can be added through the Court cards. Decide first if you want to create a musical idea using just the notes within a scale or if you want to use all the notes of a chromatic scale. For example, on a piano, you could use all the white key notes from C to C or you could use all the white and the black key notes together. To begin, separate your deck into three stacks of Major Arcana, Minor Arcana, and Court cards. Choose how many notes you wish to create. The Tarot will choose a pair of notes, chromatics, and note values.

Purpose: To create musical ideas.

Procedure: For each pair of notes do the following:
1. Pull a Major Arcana card. Find the two notes related to that card from the musical heptagram.
2. Pull a Minor Arcana card (if you want to consider chromatics). Find the natural, flat or sharp to add.
3. Pull a Court card. Refer to the note value correspondence.
4. Put the information together to create a set of notes.

The Musical Heptagram

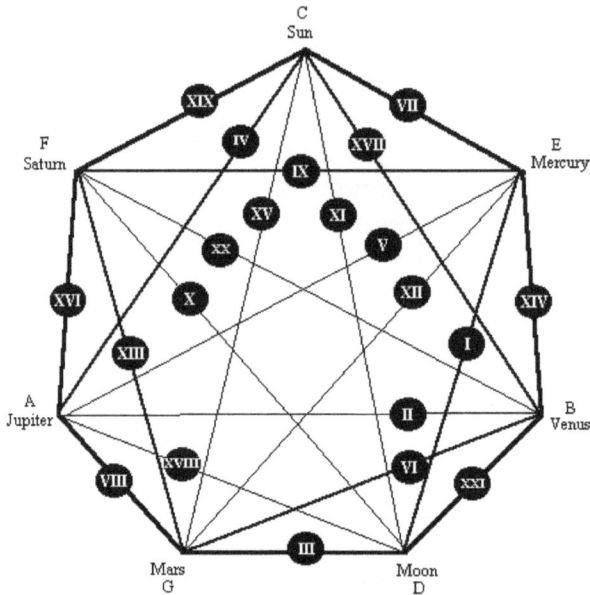

Minor Arcana Card Musical Correspondence

In this correspondence, the first five cards relate to the first note in the pair of notes while the last five relate to the second note. The table is designed to yield mostly natural notes.

Table 5.2 Note Accidental Correspondence

First Note:		Second Note:	
Ace	Flat	6	Flat
2	Natural	7	Natural
3	Natural	8	Natural
4	Natural	9	Natural
5	Sharp	10	Sharp

Table 5.3 Court Card Musical Rhythm Correspondence

Card	Rhythm
Mother of Stones	Half note, half note tied
Father of Stones	half note, half note
Daughter of Stones	half note, quarter note
Son of Stones	half note, eighth note
Mother of Swords	quarter note, tied quarter note
Father of Swords	quarter note, quarter note
Daughter of Swords	quarter note, eighth note
Son of Swords	quarter note, sixteenth note
Mother of Wands	eighth note, tied eighth note
Father of Wands	eighth note, eighth note
Daughter of Wands	eighth note, sixteenth note
Son of Wands	eighth note, quarter note
Mother of Cups	sixteenth note, tied sixteenth
Father of Cups	sixteenth note, sixteenth note
Daughter of Cups	sixteenth note, quarter note
Son of Cups	sixteenth note, eighth note
(add dots or alter rhythms as necessary to make even measures)	

Sample Reading:

Major Arcana	Minor Arcana	Court Card
VI The Lovers	2 of Swords	Son of Stones
XII The Hanged Man	6 of Cups	Son of Cups
XV The Devil	4 of Swords	Father of Swords

I chose to pick three cards which would give me six notes. The Lovers gave me the notes B and G. The 2 of Swords indicated that the two notes would be natural and the Son of Stones yielded a half note and eighth note rhythm. The Hanged Man gave me the notes E and G with the second note flatted (6 of Cups) to give me E and Gb. The rhythm is a sixteenth note followed by an eighth note (Son of Cups). I decided to add a dot to the previous eighth note (G) to make a more even rhythm. The Devil card gave me the final two notes: C and G, both as natural notes (4 of Swords) and with a rhythm of two quarter notes (Father of Swords). Because I had only room for one more eighth note in my common time measure, I changed the rhythm of the first note to an eighth note instead. The following musical example was the result.

37. Writing A Story
(a spread)

The Tarot can give you some ideas on writing a story by providing some creative possibilities for inspiration. Most every story has some common elements: some characters, a setting, a theme to the story, a conflict between the characters, a resolution, and some kind of change to the characters as a result of the conflict. With this activity you will encourage the Tarot to provide you with some clues to each of these story elements.

Purpose: To create a story.

Procedure: Pull seven cards and put in the following order.

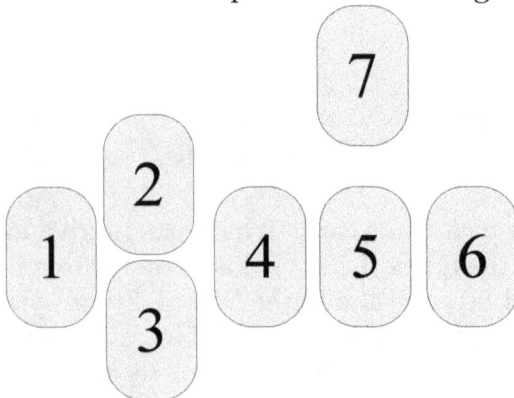

Drawing 16

Representations:
1. Setting
2. Character One
3. Character Two
4. Conflict
5. Resolution
6. Effect on the characters
7. Theme

Sample Reading:
1. Ace of Swords
2. 9 of Cups
3. The Void
4. 3 of Stones
5. 4 of Stones
6. 5 of Swords
7. 2 of Wands

The setting of my story will be a library (Ace of Swords). My first character will be a rather well-to-do gentleman (9 of Cups) and a mysterious woman (The Void). Maybe the gentleman is a paralegal doing research in the library when he meets this mysterious woman. There is a strange occurrence involving the woman which causes the man to be torn between completing his important work (3 of Stones) and following the woman to solve the mystery. He decides to risk his job and follow her. When he catches up to her, he becomes involved in her mystery and he goes into business with her as a way of resolving the mystery (4 of Stones). Unfortunately, the plan goes awry and the man begins to feel defeated (5 of Swords). The overall theme of the story is the intoxication and power of mystery (2 of Wands). It would seem the cards do not want me to write a happy story.

38. The Tarot Dance
(a correspondence)

The Tarot can be used to create dance steps in a circle dance. The practice of sacred circle dancing is becoming very popular because it is a great way to move and share together the joy of music and dance. Almost any kind of music can be used for circle dancing. With this activity, you will be able to create an original dance movement to a piece of music for a circle dance. I have designed the dance correspondence to create movements within a circle dance with the assumption that the dancers are not paired or partnered, that they will begin in a circle facing in, and that the music is in a typical common (4/4) meter. Simple adjustments can be made to change any of these assumptions. The dance will be created in sequences of 4 to 8 steps. Alterations should be made to fit together these sequences. Numbers next to directions indicate the suggested number of beats that each move should take.

Purpose: To create an original set of moves for a circle dance.

Procedure:
1. Choose a piece of music
2. Pull 4 cards to begin a dance sequence.
3. Continue to pull additional cards to complete the number of steps needed.
4. Use the dance correspondence to create your choreography.

Representations:
1. Major arcana cards indicate special moves.
2. Court cards indicate turns.
3. Minor arcana cards indicate steps.

Table 5.4 Dance Movements Correspondence – Major Arcana

Card	Movement	no. of steps
0 The Fool	jump (1)	
I The Magician	snap fingers (1)	
II The High	lift left leg and return (2)	
III The Empress	pat your left leg (1)	
IV The Emperor	pat your right leg (1)	
V Hierophant	lift right leg and return (2)	

Card	Movement	no. of steps
VI The Lovers	twirl with the person to your right (4)	
VII Chariot	twirl with the person to your left (4)	
VIII Strength	sway left and right (2)	
IX The Hermit	bend your knees and return	2
X The Wheel of Fortune	twirl right	4
XI Justice	hands out and on each other's shoulders	1
XII The Hanged Man	bend over and return	2
XIII Death	do-si-do	8
XIV Alchemy	twirl left	4
XV The Devil	clap hands	1
XVI The Tower	jump and twirl	2
XVII The Star	hands in the air	1
XVIII The Moon	lift on your toes and return	2
XIX The Sun	stamp foot	1
XX Aeon	hands behind backs of others	1
XXI The Universe	all take hands	1
0 The Multiverse	all move forward together and return	4 + 4
blank card	stand still	0

Notes:
1. With Court card Stones, dancers return to first position: facing in and hands by sides.
2. With Court card Cups, dancers face out and put hands to sides.

Table 5.5 Dance Movements Correspondence – Minor arcana

Card	Movement	no. of steps
Ace	right foot out and back	2
2	right foot out one, feet together, right foot back one, feet together.	4
3	right foot out, left foot step, left foot return, right foot return	4
4	forward three steps starting with right foot, feet together, return	8
5	left foot out and back	2
6	left foot out one, feet together, left foot back one, feet together	4
7	right foot out, left foot step, left foot return, right foot return	4
8	forward three steps starting with right foot, feet together, return	8
9	cross behind one, feet together	2
10	cross in front one, feet together	2

Table 5.6 Dance Movements Correspondence - Suits

Card	Direction
Stones	forward
Swords	right
Wands	back
Cups	left

Sample Reading:
First Four:
1. Mother of Stones
2. 5 of Stones
3. Son of Stones
4. IX The Hermit

Additional Cards:
1. Father of Wands

2. Son of Cups

I decided to create my dance with two eight beat sequences.

Sequence One (first 8 beats). The dancers will begin in a circle facing in. On beat one, they are already facing in so they will do nothing (Mother of Stones). On beats 2 and 3, the dancers will move their left foot forward and return it back (5 of Stones). Beat 4 will include another pause to complete the four beat sequence. On the next four beats the dancers will do a four beat march step (Son of Stones) to finish out the first 8 beats.

Sequence Two: (second 8 beats). Dancers will bend their knees on beat one and return on beat two (The Hermit). I needed another card to finish the next two beats so I pulled the Father of Wands which called the dancers to face out and march for two beats. I then pulled the Son of Cups and completed the second sequence by adding a turn to the center and a four beat march step. My dance sequences are complete. I can now add my dance to a piece of music by simply repeating the sequences throughout.

39. The Tarot Movie
(a discovery)

Movies began by putting together drawings and flipping through them quickly to create a sense of motion. With this activity, you will put together several cards and flip through them to create your own movie. You will need to use your imagination to make the cards connect to each other. Look all over the cards as they are being flipped to observe any connections between them. See what you can learn by observing the Tarot movie. By watching your movie carefully and letting your mind make connections between cards you may learn some interesting things or you may be inspired to create something else. The one drawback to this activity is that you may bend your cards more than you may wish so I recommend using an old deck or one that you do not mind bending a little.
<u>Purpose</u>: To create a Tarot movie.

Procedure:
  1. Pull 10 or more cards.
  2. Put them together in a stack and flip through them quickly.

40. Tarot Haiku
(a discovery)

Haiku is a short poetic form introduced by the Japanese. It consists of only three lines of poetry. The first line normally consists of five syllables, the second line of seven syllables, while the final line has five syllables. Most haiku has a natural theme or element to it. Effective haiku has two parts (two lines versus one line or one line versus two lines). The first part describes something, usually a natural element, while the second part of the poem provides an interesting new perspective on the object or setting described in the first. Since the Tarot is also full of natural settings, scenes, and elements, it can be used to inspire the creation of a haiku poem.

Purpose: To create a haiku poem.

Procedure:
  1. Pull three cards
  2. Use each card in the order pulled to create one of each of the three lines of the haiku.

Representations:
  1. First line of the haiku describing an object or setting of nature.
  2. Second line of the haiku augmenting the first or helping to prepare for the third.

Sample Reading:
  1. 5 of Cups
  2. XVII The Star
  3. I The Magician

The Five of Cups pictures two butterflies so I decided to use them as the subject for the first line. I used the image of the Star itself for the second line and the images of a large jewel in the Magician as the inspiration for the third line. Here is the haiku I created:

Two butterflies rise
Soaring upwards to the stars -
jewels in the twilight.

Chapter 6

Mars and Energy

Introduction

Mars is often thought of as the god of war but he is much more than that. His is also the symbol for the masculine, therefore he represents masculine energies. He symbolizes the awesome power and energy of the individual. If left unchecked and unbalanced by love and compassion, that energy can be turned into aggression and war. We will focus on those raw powers that Mars idealizes and can be used for making life more fun and interesting. That raw energy is also the power of our sexuality and our drive to have fun and explore. We will begin the chapter with an exploration of the energies that we can derive from Earth and then look toward how these energies can be focused on having fun and expanding sexuality.

The Energies of the Earth

41. Where Do I Find My Energy?
(a spread)

We've all experienced times when we have felt drained of energy. Sometimes it helps to know what it is that will recharge your batteries. In fact, you will use the symbols of positive and negative which you find on every battery to help find out what it is that will re-energize you.

<u>Purpose</u>: To determine what will give you energy.

<u>Procedure</u>: Pull three cards and lay out in the following spread.

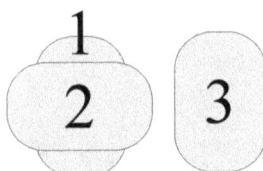

Drawing 17

<u>Representations</u>:
1. What will give you energy.
2. How you can access that energy.
3. What will drain you of energy.

<u>Sample Reading</u>:
1. Ace of Stones
2. 4 of Wands
3. 10 of Swords

I will find my energy through seeking the abundance of material things already in my life (Ace of Stones). In other words, I will be able to seek renewal from appreciating what I already have. I will be able to access that energy from seeking emotional foundations, again, by appreciating the people in my life who care for me. What will drain me is the constant worrying about the future (10 of Swords).

42. A Gemstone For Energy
(a correspondence)

Sometimes carrying around a stone of power can help you feel more energized and confident. This activity will help you determine the color of a gemstone that may help you. Although the Quest Tarot deck has gemstones included, you can use other decks to learn the needed color for your stone or other talisman.

<u>Purpose</u>: To find the color of a needed stone.

<u>Procedure</u>:

1. Pull a Minor Arcana card.
2. Compare it to the color correspondence chart.
3. Use the colors to determine the color of a stone to use.

Table 6.1 Color Correspondence

Card	Color
Ace	black
two	brown
three	gray
four	red
five	orange
six	yellow
seven	green
eight	blue
nine	purple
ten	white
Stones	very dark
Swords	medium
Wands	light
Cups	very light

Sample Reading: 8 of Stones

According to the cards, I should obtain a very dark blue stone or other object for energy.

43. Geomancy
(a correspondence)

Geomancy is an ancient divinatory technique that was based on reading signs of Earth. The original technique required the diviner to tap a number of holes in the ground in order to create a sequence of four odd or even numbers. From those numbers, patterns were created that were then used to answer questions or predict the future. With a combined system such as this you can use the best of both systems. After asking a question, you can use the four Tarot cards to give you an answer and then use the geomantic figure created to give you even more information. I have chosen to use a simple method of geomancy in relation to the Tarot for divination.

<u>Purpose</u>: To use the Tarot to produce a basic geomancy figure.

<u>Procedure</u>:
1. Pull four cards and place in a vertical line.
2. Determine if the card has an odd or even number.
3. (Court cards can be counted as Father and Son = even, Mother and Daughter = odd) (0 = even, void = odd)
4. Create a chart showing odd and even numbers as one or two dots, respectively.
5. Compare the chart to the geomancy chart below and use keywords to determine meanings.

Table 6.2 Geomancy Figures

Name	Meaning	Keyword	Figure
Puer	Boy	Strife	o o oo o
Amisio	Loss	Beyond reach	o oo o oo
Populus	People	Stability	oo oo oo oo
Fortuna Major	Great Fortune	Power	oo oo o o
Conjunctio	Conjunction	Interaction	oo o o

Name	Meaning	Keyword	Figure
			oo
Puella	Girl	Harmony	o oo o o
Rubeus	Red	Passion	oo o oo oo
Acquisitus	Gain	Success	oo o oo o
Carcer	Prison	Isolation	o oo oo o
Tristitia	Sorrow	Suffering	oo oo oo o
Laetitia	Joy	Health	o oo oo oo
Cauda Draconis	Tail of the Dragon	Ending	o o o oo
Caput Draconis	Head of the Dragon	Beginning	oo o o o
Fortuna Minor	Lesser Fortune	Swiftness	o o oo oo
Via	Way	Change	o o o o

<u>Sample Reading</u>:
1. XVII The Star (17 = odd)
2. 0 The Fool (0 = even)
3. Ace of Wands (1 = odd)
4. Daughter of Wands (odd)

The resulting figure became:
Puella (girl) - harmony

44. Energy Lines
(a discovery)

There are lines of energy that run that run through Earth. Some of these energy lines are more permanent than others. You can use the Tarot to help map out possibly fluctuating energy lines in your area or where you live. To begin, you will need to have or draw a map of the area you want to investigate. You could draw your own house to find out which room currently has the greatest energy or you could map out your work place. The map needs to be fairly large so that you can lay your Tarot cards upon it. Cards placed upon the map will describe places or lines of energy and places of grounding.

<u>Purpose</u>: To determine places of high and low energy.

<u>Procedure</u>:
1. Draw a large map or representation of a particular area.
2. Place cards onto the map in a left to right motion until the map is covered.
3. Notice the placement of Wands cards and Stones cards.
4. Mark on the map locations of greatest strength and grounding and mark lines of connection between areas of strength.

<u>Representations</u>:
1. Court cards of the Wands suit indicate energy with Ace being the greatest amount an 10 the least amount.
2. Court cards of the Stones suit indicate places of grounding with Ace being the greatest amount an 10 the least amount.

Be††er Sex

45. Kama Su†ra Posi†ions
(a correspondence)

People have been using the Kama Sutra to put some variety in sex for many years. The Kama Sutra is really more than just a manual of sexual positions. It is about how the energy of sex can be used for spiritual enlightenment but it does contain a virtual encyclopedia of sexual positions. This activity is designed to help encourage greater variety and pleasure in responsible sex between consenting adults. Such sexual activity is not something to be ashamed of - it is to be celebrated. I have put 56 positions listed in the Kama Sutra into a correspondence chart with the Minor Arcana and Court cards. The Major Arcana can be used to establish a mood or setting. In order to keep this book PG rated, I have not included any pictures or descriptions of positions. You can easily find those in any book or on-line collection.

<u>Purpose</u>: To find a sexual position to enjoy with a partner.

<u>Procedure</u>:
1. Separate out the Major Arcana cards.
2. Pull one of the remaining cards and compare to the correspondence chart.
3. Pull a Major Arcana card.

Table 6.3 Kama Sutra Correspondence - Minors

Card	Position	Card	Position	Card	Position	Card	Position
Stones:		Swords:		Wands:		Cups:	
Ace	Accordion	Ace	Boa	Ace	Elephant	Ace	Moon
Two	Alignment	Two	Butterfly	Two	Frog	Two	Nail
Three	Amazon	Three	Cat	Three	Goddess	Three	Octopus
Four	Andromaque	Four	Column	Four	Indra	Four	Oyster
Five	Antelope	Five	Courtesan	Five	Lotus	Five	Plough

Card	Position	Card	Position	Card	Position	Card	Position
Six	Anvil	Six	Cow	Six	Lover	Six	Reed
Seven	Astride	Seven	Crab	Seven	Magpie	Seven	Scissors
Eight	Balance	Eight	Dance	Eight	Mill	Eight	Scorpion
Nine	Bamboo	Nine	Dog	Nine	Missionary	Nine	Seesaw
Ten	Bee	Ten	Eagle	Ten	Monkey	Ten	Semblance

Table 6.4 Kama Sutra Correspondence - Court Cards

Card	Position
Queen of Stones	Slav
King of Stones	Spoon
Daughter of Stones	Star
Son of Stones	Stem
Queen of Swords	Suspended
King of Swords	Thighs
Daughter of Swords	Tiger
Son of Swords	Tree
Queen of Wands	Turtle
King of Wands	Wheel
Daughter of Wands	Wheelbarrow
Son of Wands	Wide Open
Queen of Cups	Wide V
King of Cups	Willow
Daughter of Cups	Wolf
Son of Cups	Yin Yang

Sample Reading:
1. 2 of Cups
2. XXI The Universe

The chosen position is called the Nail (2 of Cups) and the setting is outside at night where we can view the cosmos (The Universe). Excuse me while I go chill a bottle of champagne...

46. Sexual Fantasy
(a spread)

A technique that is often suggested to couples to help spice up their sex life is to use fantasy and role-play. Lovers are encouraged to take on the roles of other characters or situations. The Tarot can be used to help create these characters. You can use all the cards or separate out only those cards which have people shown on them. Use your imagination to create two characters. Decide how they would meet each other and then engage in lovemaking. You could go so far as to meet each other at a certain location and actually pretend to meet and pick each other up then head off to some romantic location.

<u>Purpose</u>: To encourage fantasy in sexual activity.

<u>Procedure</u>:
1. Pull two cards.
2. Create characters based on the cards.
3. Go have fun being those characters.

<u>Sample Reading</u>:
1. Ace of Wands
2. 2 of Swords

The two characters here could be a rather suave passionate person who thinks s/he is some kind of Don (or Donna) Juan (Ace of Wands). The second character could be a peace-loving hippy type (2 of Swords). In a possible scenario, the two meet at a bar. The lover could come on strong at first to the hippy who rebukes him/her for a time but, of course, eventually gives in. What were the magic words the lover used to finally convince the hippy? Use your imagination.

47. Sex Game
(a game)

One way to bring more fun and excitement into a positive sexual relationship is to play a sex game. This one can be played with two or more people. You can, of course, change the tables to suit your own needs, interests, fantasies, and limits. I suggest you first review the game and make any changes before beginning play. You will need to separate out the Major Arcana cards and make a stack for each of the four suits of the remaining cards. The game will also need some equipment (besides the cards, of course) depending on which activities you include. The equipment that may be needed includes chips or tokens, a feather, a 30 second timer, and some soft restraints. The use of tokens allows people to make choices about their play.

<u>Purpose</u>: To generate more fun in a consenting adult sexual relationship through playing a game.

<u>Procedure</u>:
1. Set the five stacks of cards on the table. It may help to identify the stacks. Each of the four suits and the Major Arcana cards has a specific purpose.
   a) Wands = Action cards
   b) Swords = Clothing cards
   c) Stones = Parts Of The Body cards
   d) Cups = Take A Chance cards
   e) Major Arcana = Winner cards
2. Give each player three tokens.
3. Each player is given a Winner card and turns it over one at a time. The person with the highest card is the Giver and the person with the lowest card is the Receiver.
4. The Giver takes an action card and turns it over. If the cards is an Ace (undress) card, the Giver turns over a Clothing card. Otherwise the Giver turns over a Body Part card. The resulting action is called the Gift.
5. The Giver must make on of two choices:
6. Offer the Gift to the Receiver, or
7. Give a token to the Receiver (unless you have none).

8. The Receiver must make one of four choices:
   a) Accept the Gift from the Giver.
   b) Deny the Gift and give a token to the Giver (unless you have none);
   c) Take a Chance card; or
   d) Remove a piece of clothing.
9. Begin the next round by collecting all Winner cards, shuffling and passing one out to each player again.

Table 6.5 Sex Game Correspondences – Wands and Swords

Wands: Action cards		Swords: Clothing cards	
Ace	undress	Ace	shoes
2	kiss	2	socks
3	caress	3	stockings
4	suck	4	pants
5	tease	5	skirt
6	lick	6	underpants
7	massage	7	undershirt
8	tickle	8	shirt
9	blow on	9	sweater, jacket, etc.
10	be flattered	10	bra
Mother	feather	Mother	belt
Father	nibble	Father	hat
Daughter	free choice of loser	Daughter	free choice of Receiver
Son	free choice of winner	Son	free choice of Giver

Table 6.6 Sex Game Correspondences – Stones and Cups

Stones: Body Parts cards		Cups: Take A Chance cards	
Ace	feet	Ace	take one token from Giver
2	legs	2	take two tokens from Giver
3	hips	3	give two tokens to Giver
4	genitals	4	give two tokens to anyone
5	stomach	5	seductively remove an item of clothing
6	back	6	put on a piece of clothing
7	chest	7	be seductive for 30 seconds
8	shoulders	8	seductively tease someone for 30 seconds
9	neck	9	restrain and tease someone for 30 seconds
10	head	10	be restrained and teased for 30 seconds
Mother	ears	Mother	winner proceeds with action card
Father	lips	Father	all players pick action card
Daughter	free choice of loser	Daughter	free card - no action
Son	free choice of winner	Son	free card - no action

Additional Rules:

1. Only exposed articles of clothing can be removed. For

example, underwear cannot be removed if there are pants or a skirt still covering them.

2. If a player has no tokens, one of the other choices must be taken.

Sample Play: (2 players)

Player 1 picks XVIII The Moon; player 2 picks II The High Priestess. Player 1 is the Giver and Player 2 is the Receiver. Player 1 chooses an Action Card and pulls the Mother of Wands and then pulls a Body Part card - the Father of Stones. The Gift will be to feather the lips of Player 2. Player 1 decides to offer the Gift to player 2 rather than just pay one token. Player 2 knows how ticklish that feather is so declines the gift and must now either pay the Giver a token, take a Chance card or remove a piece of clothing. From earlier play, Player 2 has lost all chips so now only has two remaining choices. Player 2 decides to take a Chance card and pulls the Mother of Cups which calls the Giver to proceed anyway. Player 2 gets feathered lips (and loves it!)

Fun

48. Which Game Should I Play?
(a correspondence)

Tarot cards, like any other card set, can be used to play games. And why not? Not everything that is done with the Tarot has to be serious and dead-pan. Why not keep an old deck out just for playing games as well? Just about everyone loves to play games but sometimes you just do not know which one to play. With the Tarot, you can assign games to the cards and let it choose for you. In the Appendix to this book are 14 original games for Tarot cards. You can use the list here to choose one to play or change the list to include your own favorite games. Then, gather some folks together for a fun time and play the game. For this correspondence you will only use Minor Arcana and Court cards.

Purpose: To find a game to play based on the list in this book's appendix.

<u>Procedure</u>:
1. Pull a Minor Arcana or Court card
2. Refer to the Game Correspondence below.
3. Find the game in the Appendix and play it.

Table 6.7 Tarot Game Correspondence

Card	Game
Ace	Classic Tarot
2	Tahtzee
3	Tarot Strategy
4	Cosmic Twenty One
5	The Great Pyramid
6	At The Races
7	Squad Attack
8	Dungeon
9	Tarot Bowling
10	Out!
Son	Tarot Baseball
Daughter	Bluff
Father	Tarot Golf
Mother	Tarot Towers

49. Which Sport Should I Play?
(a correspondence)

Sports games can also be assigned to cards in the same way that cards can be assigned to card games.

<u>Purpose</u>: To choose a sports activity.

<u>Procedure</u>: Assign your favorite sports activities to each of the Major

Arcana and pull a card to choose which one to do.

50. Tarot Improv
(a spread)

Improvisational comedy is fast becoming a popular form of entertainment. The idea is to create situations, characters, and resolutions on the spot. It can be a challenging and fun activity. With the Tarot, you can create a variety of unusual characters and situations to be used for creating improvisational scenes. This activity assumes two players though any number of people could be added to the activity.

Purpose: To create characters and situation for improvisational comedy sketches.

Procedure:
1. Pull five cards and place in the following spread.
2. Determine the qualities of the characters and situation they are in.
3. Pull additional cards if needed to define the situation.

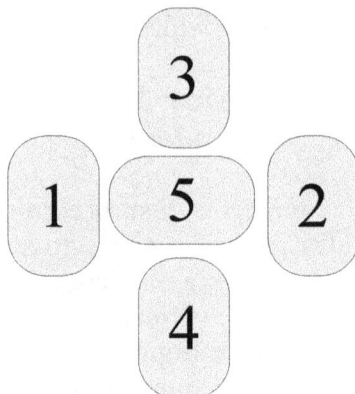

Drawing 18

Representations:
1. The current scene
2. Where the scene is headed.
3. The first character.
4. The second character.
5. The complication

Sample Reading:
1. Daughter of Cups
2. Hierophant
3. 2 of Stones
4. XVII The Star
5. 5 of Stones

In this scene created by the cards, the first character is a young emotional female (Daughter of Cups) while the other character is a wise old teacher (Hierophant). Characters could be played by either gender. They are both in agreement about wanting something (2 of Stones) that they were hoping to get (The Star) but they are short of money (5 of Stones). I pulled another card to find out what it is they want to get and got XII The Hanged Man. I decided that what they wanted was some magic rope and that they needed to convince a store owner why he or she should sell either one of them the rope at below cost. Our two characters can now begin improvising the scene.

Chapter 7

Jupiter and Transcendence

Introduction

The planet Jupiter is associated with expansion and philosophy. In the Roman pantheon, Jupiter was the master of all the other gods. In this chapter, we will honor Jupiter by exploring ways in which the Tarot can be used as an aid in spiritual growth and to expand the divination qualities of the Tarot by combining it with other divination systems.

Spiritual Growth

51. Where Am I Spiritually?
(a spread)

It is easy to feel like you have become stuck in your spiritual journey. You may have felt like you were moving along very well. You were learning and discovering things about yourself and the universe and then, all of a sudden, it all seemed to stop and you feel like you are revving your wheels in the mud and going nowhere fast. You should know that this is a natural part of the growth process. Everyone has time when their development slows down or even halts for a time before the next growth spurt occurs. Sometimes, though, that being stuck feeling can last much longer than it should. In those times it helps to know where you are on the journey and what you should do next to move ahead. With this simple spread you can find out those things. It is based on the theory that the Major Arcana cards describe the complete spiritual journey in all its steps. If you were to lay out your Major Arcana cards in numerical order you would come to understand the progression of a spiritual path. Remember, though, that the cards do not actually describe a straight line with an ending. The last Major Arcana card (the Multiverse in the Quest deck) is followed by the first card (The Fool) to create a complete cycle. The path of spiritual knowledge is never fully completed. Spiritual enlightenment is a never ending unfolding of truth and expanding awareness.

Purpose: To discover where you are on the spiritual journey.

Procedure:
1. Separate your Major Arcana cards out from the rest of the deck.
2. Pull a Major Arcana card.
3. Find the next numerical Major Arcana card.
4. Pull a card from the other cards.
5. Place them in the following spread.

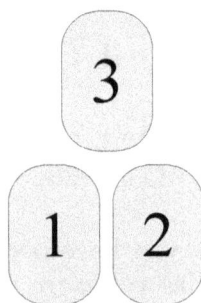

Drawing 19

Representations:
1. Where you are in the spiritual journey.
2. The next step in the journey (your goal).
3. What you can do to get you there.

Sample Reading:
1. XVI The Tower

2. XVII The Star
3. Mother of Wands

I pulled the Tower card and then found the very next card in the order of Major Arcana cards which is the Star card. Then I pulled a non-Major Arcana card. I seem to be stuck in my journey on old, worn out beliefs and customs (The Tower). To move on, I will need to gain a sense of hope, wonder, and renewal (The Star). To get me there and out of my rut I will need to seek the advice of a creative woman (Mother of Wands).

52. The Labyrinth of the Tarot
(a discovery)

This is a very effective and powerful meditation that I often use with my students and in workshops. It combines the Major Arcana's description of the spiritual journey with the process of inner contemplation derived from the labyrinth. A labyrinths is a circuitous path that leads someone into its inner sanctum. It is different than a maze in that there are no attempts to trick you by offering choices in direction. There is only one path to the center and out again. Labyrinths have been used for centuries to encourage a pilgrim to seek inner understanding and contemplation. A simple labyrinth can be made using the major Arcana cards to create stations within and along a pathway to the center of a structure design. As you progress into the labyrinth you can stop at each Major Arcana card and use it to meditate upon its spiritual message.

Purpose: To create a path of spiritual exploration and contemplation.

Procedure:
1. Build the labyrinths using the Major Arcana cards in the design below.
2. Either take the included list of possible questions or choose your own questions for each Major Arcana card.
3. Enter the labyrinths and stop at each card in numerical order. Consider a question or just meditate upon the card.
4. Continue through the labyrinths until you reach the middle.

Meditate.

5. Exit the labyrinths in the opposite direction in which you entered it.

The Labyrinth Design

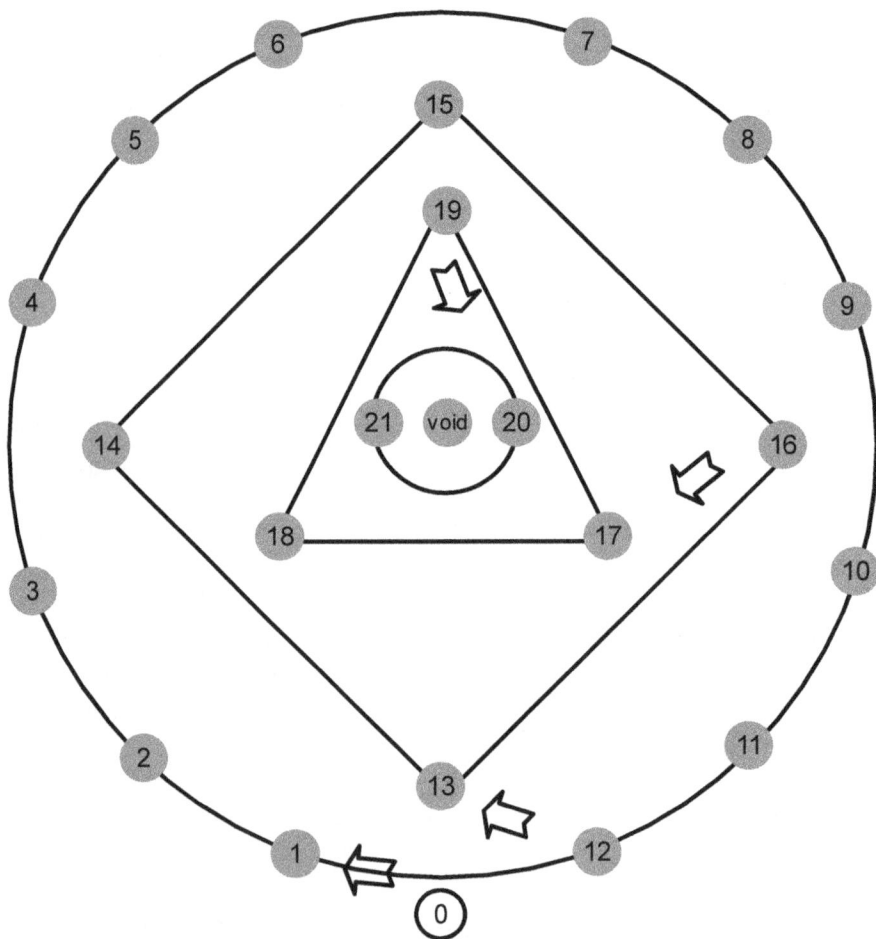

Table 7.1 Possible Labyrinth Questions

position	no.	card	question
outside	0	Fool	how can I be open to new beginnings?
outer circle:	1	Magician	what is the role of the God in daily life?
	2	High Priestess	what is the role of the Goddess in daily life?
	3	Empress	what is the role of the mother?
	4	Emperor	what is the role of the father?
	5	Hierophant	how can I make a change for the better?
	6	Lovers	how can I learn to be more loving?
	7	Chariot	what is my direction?
	8	Strength	how can justice be sought in relationships?
	9	Hermit	when is silence needed more often?
	10	Wheel of Fortune	what is the role of change?
	11	Justice	what desires are necessary, unnecessary?
	12	Hanged Man	what can I sacrifice for greater good?
square:	13	Death	what do I need to end or bring back to life?
	14	Alchemy	how does creativity play a role in my life?
	15	Devil	how can I regain a sense of joy and fun?
	16	Tower	what is keeping me from progressing in life?
triangle:	17	Star	what do I hope for? Is it worthwhile and realistic?
	18	Moon	how can I nurture my feminine side?
	19	Sun	how can I foster my masculine side?
layers:	20	Aeon	where do I need to apply patience & understanding?
	21	Universe	where do I need to find wholeness and unity in life?
center		Void	how can I embrace silence and emptiness?

53. Finding A Teacher
(a spread)

It is said that when the student is ready the teacher will come. That may be true but sometimes you need a little help knowing when and where that teacher will be. The teacher may come but what if you are not there to greet him or her? This spread is very similar to the one on finding a romantic partner but with an added card and is designed to help you meet up and recognize a spiritual teacher.

Purpose: To help find a spiritual teacher.

Procedure: Pull six cards in the pattern below.

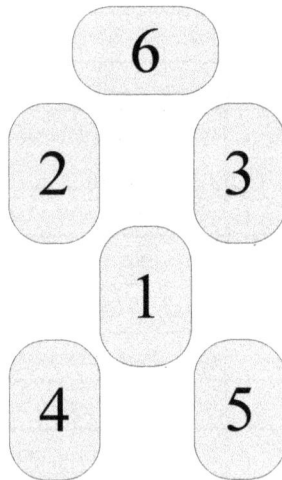

Drawing 20

Representations:
1. A clue as to who the person is.
2. Where you should go to meet this person.
3. What you should be doing.
4. How you should approach the person.
5. How to know if you have found the right person.
6. What he or she is meant to teach you.

<u>Sample Reading:</u>
1. 3 of Swords
2. V Hierophant
3. Daughter of Wands
4. 6 of Cups
5. VII Chariot
6. 5 of Cups

The teacher I seek is a creative thinker (3 of Swords). I will need to find her in a class or lecture setting (Hierophant). I will need to be energetic and seek her out through asking a lot of questions (Daughter of Wands) and I should approach her with joy in my heart (6 of Cups). I will know she is the right person because of her determination and strength in her convictions (Chariot). She will teach me how to overcome disappointment and remain committed to my path (5 of Cups).

54. Moral Decision Making
(a discovery)

We have to make hundreds of decisions every day and some are easier than others. Some decisions involve choosing where to go to eat or which lane you will drive in while other decisions involve making life changes. The bigger decisions tend to be spiritual in nature. That is, they are related to how we see ourselves and our role in the universe. Some are moral decisions and involve considering how to act within your own ethical guidelines. In this activity, you will go through the steps of making a moral decision. You can use the cards to represent the elements involved in these steps either through chance or through choosing the cards. The key to making any major decision is to determine the truth of a situation. People may have many ideas of what a problem may be but it is important to discover the actual underlying problem. If you are certain of knowing the answer to any part of this activity then choose a card to represent that understanding. Otherwise, pull a card and let the deck tell you the true answer. I learned this process from a friend and mentor of mine and I am in debt to her for her guidance.

<u>Purpose</u>: To aid you in making moral decisions.

<u>Procedure</u>:
1. Determine answers to the following questions:
    a) What is the actual problem?
    b) Whose problem is it?
    c) What options are available to solve the problem? (try to find at least three)
    d) What are the consequences of each option?
    e) What values do I hold that are relevant to this decision?
    f) Which of the consequences most closely fits my values?
2. Either choose or pull cards to represent answers to each of these questions.
3. Lay cards out in order of the questions and determine the best action.

55. Life Lessons
(a correspondence)

There are many lessons to be learned in life but some are important for all of us to learn. In this activity, you can determine which of these important life lessons are needed for you at this time.

<u>Purpose</u>: To determine which life lesson is needed.

<u>Procedure</u>:
1. Separate the Major Arcana cards.
2. Pull a Major Arcana card.
3. Pull a card from the remainder of the deck (Minor Arcana and Court cards).
4. Set them next to each other.
5. Relate the Major Arcana to the correspondence below.

<u>Representations</u>:
1. The life lesson that is needed.
2. How that lesson should be applied.

Table 7.2 Life Lesson Correspondence

Card	Correspondence
0 The Fool	Learn to take control of your reactions
I The Magician	Learn to create your own magick
II The High Priestess	Learn to find wholeness of self
III The Empress	Learn to be engaged in life.
IV The Emperor	Learn to take action
V Hierophant	Learn to seek the simple solution
VI The Lovers	Learn to keep commitments
VII Chariot	Learn to accept change
VIII Strength	Learn to accept disappointment
IX The Hermit	Learn to find your center and sense of self-worth
X The Wheel of Fortune	Learn how to bounce back
XI Justice	Learn to forgive
XII The Hanged Man	Learn from to accept and grow from crisis
XIII Death	Learn to accept sadness
XIV Alchemy	Learn to seek meaning in all things
XV The Devil	Learn to find the humor in things
XVI The Tower	Learn to be responsible
XVII The Star	Learn to find lessons every day
XVIII The Moon	Learn to follow your dreams
XIX The Sun	Learn your own source of inner light and let it shine
XX Aeon	Learn to accept mistakes
XXI The Universe	Learn the unity of all living things
0 The Multiverse	Learn to separate from your ego
Void	Learn to embrace mystery

Sample Reading:
  1. XVII The Star

2. Father of Cups

The life lesson that is most relevant to me today is to learn to find lessons in every day (The Star) so I will need to be aware of what today will teach me. I will need to apply that lesson to a spiritual man that I know (Father of Cups).

Divination

56. Tarot and Astrology
(a correspondence and a spread)

If you have ever had your astrological natal chart done then you have looked at those complicated astrological diagrams and wondered how anyone makes sense of those things. It may help to have a better model for your chart. You can use the Tarot to depict the planets, signs, and houses in a natal chart. By using cards, you can easily remove things and put them back to simplify your view of the chart. It can also be easier to observe all those aspects as well. By using the correspondence below, Major Arcana cards can be used to represent planets and signs while the numbers of the Minor Arcana can represent the houses (using Father and Mother for houses 11 and 12).

Table 7.3 Planets and Signs Correspondence

Card	Correspondence
0 The Fool	Uranus
I The Magician	Pisces
II The High Priestess	Jupiter
III The Empress	Neptune
IV The Emperor	Saturn
V Hierophant	Mars
VI The Lovers	Venus
VII Chariot	Cancer
VIII Strength	Libra
IX The Hermit	Virgo
X The Wheel of Fortune	Gemini
XI Justice	Leo
XII The Hanged Man	Aries
XIII Death	Scorpio
XIV Alchemy	Sagittarius
XV The Devil	Capricorn
XVI The Tower	Taurus
XVII The Star	Mercury
XVIII The Moon	Moon
XIX The Sun	Sun
XX Aeon	Aquarius
XXI The Universe	Pluto

The Tarot can also be combined with astrology to provide another system of divination. A simple method would be to pull a card for each of the 12 astrological houses. You would seek the answer to your question by looking at the house that most closely related to your question and then observe the card in that house. Another more complicated way would be to use the Major Arcana cards and pull one card that represented one of the planets and another that represented one of the signs and place them in the house related to your question. You would then read your answer as [planet] in [sign] in the [house]. You would need to know the meaning of all the signs and planets to do this method, of course. I will illustrate the simpler method here.

<u>Purpose</u>: To use astrology as an aid in divination.

<u>Procedure</u>:
1. Decide on a question for divination.
2. Set out 10 Minor Arcana cards and a Mother and Father card in a circle to represent the 12 astrological houses.
3. Pull a card for each house.
4. Compare the meaning of the card to the meaning of the house. Determine which house would best answer your question and observe the card in that house.

Table 7.4 Meanings of the Houses

House	Keyword	Focus
1st	Self	The area of life dealing with establishment of personal identity.
2nd	Possessions	The area of life dealing with resources and material security.
3rd	Communication	The area of life dealing with communication; relationship to the environment.
4th	Home	The area of life dealing with imagination; domestic life.
5th	Pleasure and Creativity	The area of life dealing with finding joy, pleasure, and creative expression.
6th	Health	The area of life dealing with work and feeling talented and useful.
7th	Partnerships	The area of life dealing with personal relationships and intimacy.
8th	Change	The area of life dealing with cycles and the mystical.
9th	Philosophy	The area of life dealing with changes, exploration, and learning.
10th	Career	The area of life dealing with avocation, life purpose, and destiny.
11th	Friendships	The area dealing with life goals, and association with friends and groups.
12th	Subconscious	The area of life dealing with the personality from within.

57. Automatic Writing
(discovery)

Automatic writing is a divination method in which you simply begin to write on a piece of paper and let yourself write anything that comes to your mind. You must continue writing for at least a minute or more without stopping or looking back over what you are writing. The hardest part of doing automatic writing is in starting. By pulling a Tarot card you can provide yourself a place in which to start as you use the card for inspiration.

Purpose: To use automatic writing as an aid in divination.

Procedure:
1. Get several pieces of paper and a pen in front of you.
2. Pull a card from the deck.
3. Begin writing your thoughts and feelings about the card.
4. Continue to write without stopping for at least a minute.
5. Look over what you have written for clues to lessons or answers you need.

58. Tarot Rune Stones
(a discovery)

One of my teachers used rune stones when reading the Tarot. The Runes are a very powerful divination system and I have always wondered if the Tarot and the runes could be combined into one system. I created this idea of the Tarot rune stones. It combines the 25 stones of the Elder Futhark runes and 10 stones in each of the four elements to create 65 stones. You will need to make or collect your own blank stones in five colors and then add designs to them.

Purpose: To use the runes and stones representing minor stones as an aid in divination.

Procedure:
1. Obtain stones in the following number and color:
   a) 10 yellow stones (for Air)
   b) 10 red stones (for Fire)
   c) 10 blue stones (for Water)
   d) 10 green stones (for Earth)
   e) 25 purple stones (for Spirit and runes)
2. On each of the 10 elemental stones, paint the following symbols to represent the numbers from one to ten.
3. Pull a number of stones in the same manner as you might any tarot spread.

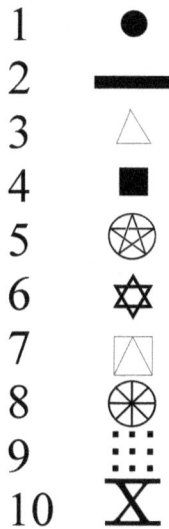

1	●
2	▬
3	△
4	■
5	⊗
6	✡
7	◹
8	⊕
9	⦂⦂
10	X

Drawing 21

59. Tarot I-Ching
(a spread)

The I-Ching is a divination system that is very ancient. It uses a set of closed or broken lines to create a binary system. Six of these lines are combined together to create a hexagram which is used to make a divinatory reading. In this activity, the basis of the I-Ching system is used to create a Tarot I-Ching.

<u>Purpose</u>: To use I-Ching figures as an aid in divination.

<u>Procedure</u>:
1. Pull six cards and stack in a vertical line from bottom to top.
2. On a piece of paper,
    a) mark a straight line (___) for even numbers
    b) a broken line (_ _) for odd numbers.
    c) Zeros count as even numbers.
3. Create a hexagram and observe its meaning. This is the primary figure.

4. Court cards are transitionary cards. Mothers and Daughters are marked as broken lines and Fathers and Sons are marked as solid lines. A second figure called the relating figure can be created by changing all Court cards to opposite lines and re-drawing the complete hexagram.
5. Each of the six cards of the hexagram can also be read for further meaning.

6

5

4

3

2

1

Drawing
22

Representations:
1. Inner trigram: the entrance - the inner root of the problem
2. Inner trigram: the center - the inner focus of the problem
3. Inner trigram: the transition - from inner to outer
4. Outer trigram: the manifestation - how the problem manifests outward
5. Outer trigram: the center - the outer focus of the problem
6. Outer trigram: the exit - how the problem appears to others
7. The primary figure represents the current situation or condition.
8. The relating figure represents a likely change to the situation.

Find the inner trigram or the pattern created by the first three cards and then the outer trigram from the last three cards. Stack the inner trigram below the outer trigram. Find the number that relates to both the inner and outer trigram and then read the divination of the number of that hexagram below.

Table 7.5 I-Ching Trigrams

Outer Trigram: Inner Trigram:	☰	☳	☵	☶	☷	☴	☲	☱
☰	1	11	34	5	26	9	14	43
☳	12	2	16	8	23	20	35	45
☵	25	24	51	3	27	42	21	17
☶	6	7	40	29	4	59	64	47
☷	33	15	62	39	52	53	56	31
☴	44	46	32	48	18	57	50	28
☲	13	36	55	63	22	37	30	49
☱	10	19	54	60	41	61	38	58

Table 7.6 I-Ching Hexagrams

Number	Keyword	Meaning
1	Force	strength, creative energy, action
2	Field	yield, nourish, provide
3	Sprouting	beginning of growth
4	Enveloping	immature, young, unaware
5	Attending	wait for, wait on, watch
6	Arguing	dispute, controversy, conflict
7	Legions	discipline, organize, lead
8	Grouping	alliance, support, gather
9	Small Accumulating	adapt, nurture, collect
10	Treading	find your way, support
11	Pervading	prosper, expand, communicate
12	Obstruction	obstacle, block, cut-off
13	Concording People	harmony, cooperation
14	Great Possessions	concentrate, achievements, results
15	Humbling	be simple, fundamental principles
16	Providing For	enjoyment, gathering tools
17	Following	accept guidance, go with the flow
18	Corruption	disorder, decay, new path
19	Nearing	approach, new arrival
20	Viewing	contemplate, divination, step back
21	Gnawing	confront, be tenacious, reveal
22	Adorning	embellish, beautify, courage
23	Stripping	eliminate waste, worn out

Number	Keyword	Meaning
24	Returning	renewal, re-birth, hope
25	Without Embroiling	disentangle, spontaneity, purity
26	Great Accumulating	concentrate, focus, unite
27	Jaws	nourish, take things in, speaking
28	Great Exceeding	crisis, forcefulness, idealism
29	Repeating the Gorge	danger, dive in, practice
30	Radiance	light, warmth, awareness
31	Conjoining	action, connection, excite
32	Persevering	continue, endure, constant
33	Retiring	withdraw, retreat, conceal
34	Great Invigorating	strength, purpose, go forward
35	Prospering	advance, receive, promotion
36	Hiding Brightness	protection, acceptance, modesty
37	Dwelling People	adapt, support, family
38	Diverging	opposition, discord, change
39	Difficulties	confrontation, oppression, affliction
40	Loosening	solve problems, liberation, freedom
41	Diminishing	loss, decrease, sacrifice
42	Augmenting	increase, expand, develop
43	Deciding	breakthrough, judgment, reveal
44	Coupling	opening, welcoming, sex
45	Clustering	gather, collect, crowds
46	Ascending	rise, advance, new level

Number	Keyword	Meaning
47	Confining	restriction, truthful, turn inward
48	The Well	interact, network, nourish
49	Skinning	moult, reveal, revolt
50	The Vessel	consecrate, drink in, contain
51	Shake	shock, stir up, forceful
52	Bound	calm, boundary, limits
53	Gradual Advancing	approach, adapt, penetrate
54	Converting	hidden potential, passion, uncontrollable change
55	Abounding	culmination, generosity, fullness
56	Sojourning	wandering, exile, quest
57	Gentle Penetrating	flexible, acceptance, influence
58	Open	self-expression, joy, exchange
59	Dispersing	dissolve, clear up, scatter
60	Articulating	limit, speak, define
61	Center	connection, sincerity, spirituality
62	Small Exceeding	adapt, careful, transition
63	Already Fording	in progress, order, proceeding
64	Not Yet Fording	possibility, patience, revelation

Sample Reading:

1. Father of Stones   (___) transitional
2. 5 of Swords   (_ _)
3. 3 of Wands   (_ _)
4. Daughter of Stones   (_ _) transitional
5. Father of Cups   (___) transitional
6. XIV Alchemy   (___)

The hexagram is derived by reading from card one up to card six. The resulting pattern then becomes:

Primary Figure: Relating Figure:

____   _ _
____   _ _
_ _   Outer trigram   _ _
_ _   ____
_ _   _ _
____   Inner trigram   ____

The resulting number from the chart is 42 which is the hexagram titled Augmenting. A reading can be made from that hexagram as well as from the position of the six cards themselves. Since there are some transitionary (Court) cards, a second relating figure can be drawn which results in hexagram number 36 titled Hiding Brightness.

60. Tarot and the Pendulum
(a discovery)

The pendulum can be used quite effectively with the Tarot to create a way to make a choice. Tarot cards can be used to represent a wide variety of things which can then be set in an array. The pendulum can then be used to indicate one of these cards and the choice that needs to be made. There are times when only a few choices need to be made and an entire deck of cards is not limited enough to make the needed decision. You could certainly just reduce the number of cards to a small amount and then pick one card but with the pendulum, your subconscious mind is more involved on making the actual choice. In this activity, you will use five cards to represent 5 possible choices and then employ your pendulum to make the final choice.

Purpose: To use the pendulum as a guide in divination.

Procedure:
   1. Pull or choose 5 cards to represent the possible choices in a

given situation.
2. Spread the cards in a semicircle.
3. Begin with the pendulum in the middle of the cards and allow it to swing towards the needed answer.

Illustration 1

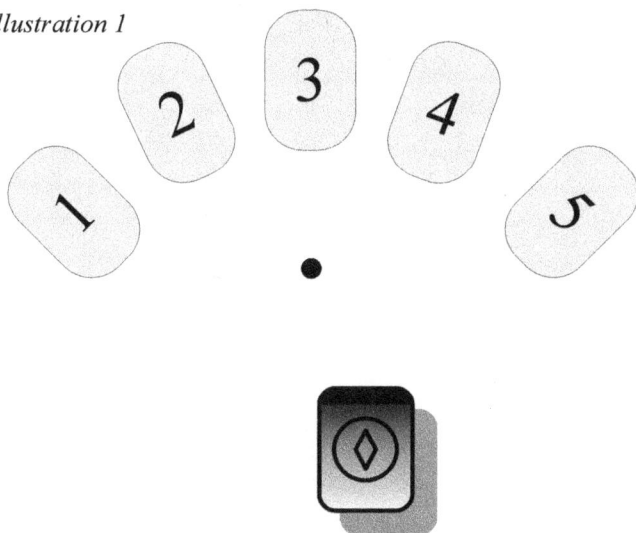

Chapter 8

Saturn and Limitations

Introduction

aturn was once considered the last planet in the solar system and thus became known as the planet of boundaries and limitations. Beyond Saturn was the great mysterious realm of the stars. One of the limits of our own physical self is our health. Without strong bodies, minds, hearts, and souls, we are hampered in the move forward on our life path. The world also has its limitations; they are of time and space. All our physical actions are limited by the available space and environment and by the restraints of time. The planet Saturn also reminds us to limit our own selves. The pursuit of unrestrained desires without the consideration its effects upon ourselves and of the needs and rights of others can threaten the health, well-being, and safety of all of us. In order to prevent this, we must be able to determine our own limits and set boundaries between ourselves and others.

Health

61. Chakra Balancing
(a spread)

In this activity, you will allow the cards to determine the condition of each of your seven main chakras plus three additional chakras. The cards will tell you whether each is balanced or unbalanced. Knowledge of the chakras and methods to balance these wheels of energy would be helpful in following through with this activity although the cards will also give you some clue as how balancing may be done.

<u>Purpose</u>: To determine the condition of the chakras.

<u>Procedure</u>:
1. Shuffle the deck and pull ten cards to lay face down in the spread below.
2. Flip the top card of the deck and do one of the following:
   a) If the card is a Minor Arcana, put it in the numbered location of the spread face up.
   b) If the card is not a Minor Arcana, lay it horizontally on the first card location that has not been covered by a face up card and follows the last placed face down card. For example: If the card turned over from the deck is a 7 of Stones and the face down card in position 7 has no face up card upon it, that 7 of Stones would be placed in the 7th chakra position face up. If there was a face up card there, it would be placed horizontally face down on the root chakra position unless the last card placed horizontally was put there. In that case, the 7 of Stones would be placed in the next chakra position (number 2).
3. Continue to do step B until all the Minor Arcana cards have been placed face up in their location.

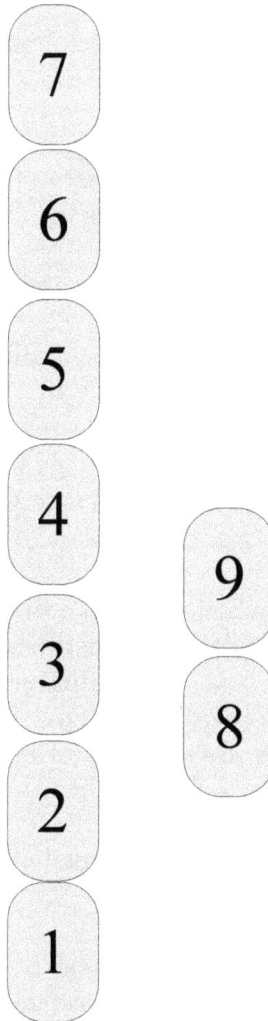

7

6

5

4

9

3

8

2

1

Drawing 23

Representations:

1. Root Chakra
2. Spleen Chakra
3. Solar Plexus Chakra
4. Heart Chakra
5. Throat Chakra

6. Third Eye Chakra
7. Crown Chakra
8. Feet Chakra
9. Hand Chakra
10. Aural Chakra (above the crown)
    a) Face up cards indicate strength of chakra.
    b) Cups and Swords = balanced, Stones = under charged, Wands = over charged
    c) First face down cards represent what can be done to balance that chakra.
    d) Horizontal face down cards indicate the strength of the imbalance or balance.
(more cards = greater strength)

62. Which Therapy?
(a correspondence)

We all have times when we need a little help getting our bodies and minds back into balance but sometimes it is hard to know just which therapy would be best. With this activity, you can allow the cards to help you discover which therapy might be best for a minor problem or imbalance. As always, if you are suffering from a major health ailment, consult your doctor or health practitioner first.

Purpose: To determine the therapy needed at this time.

Procedure:
1. Separate out the Major Arcana cards.
2. Pull a Major Arcana card and relate it to the correspondence chart below.

Table 8.1 Therapy Correspondence

Card	Therapy
0 The Fool	play
I The Magician	spiritual healing
II The High Priestess	ritual
III The Empress	herbalism
IV The Emperor	medical doctor
V Hierophant	study
VI The Lovers	massage/ hug
VII Chariot	acupressure/ acupuncture
VIII Strength	ayurveda
IX The Hermit	meditation
X The Wheel of Fortune	movement/ dance/ exercise
XI Justice	chakra balancing
XII The Hanged Man	yoga
XIII Death	past life regression
XIV Alchemy	art
XV The Devil	reiki/ energy work
XVI The Tower	sound/ music
XVII The Star	homeopathy
XVIII The Moon	nature/ shaman
XIX The Sun	psychology
XX Aeon	mindfulness
XXI The Universe	color
0 The Multiverse	aromatherapy
blank card	retreat/ rest

63. Elemental Assessment
(a spread)

When you are not quite sure what ails you, this activity can help you zero in on what you need to focus upon to feel balanced and whole by letting you observe the strength of each of the four parts of your self and your spiritual strength as well.

<u>Purpose</u>: To discover what may be causing unbalance in your life.

<u>Procedure</u>:
1. Pull a card and place face up on each of the four elemental locations and another in the center for Spirit. (See the spread pattern below).
2. Continue to do A above until all the positions contain one card related to the element of that card's position. Stones = Earth, Swords = Air, Wands = Fire, Cups = Water, Major Arcana = Spirit
3. Assess the strength of each elemental area. Earth = body, Air = mind, Fire = heart, Water = soul, Spirit = spiritual connection, Ace = most healthy, 10 = least healthy, XXI = strong spiritual connection, Fool = weak spiritual connection, Court cards indicate people who may causing difficulties cards underneath may help to find balance in that element.

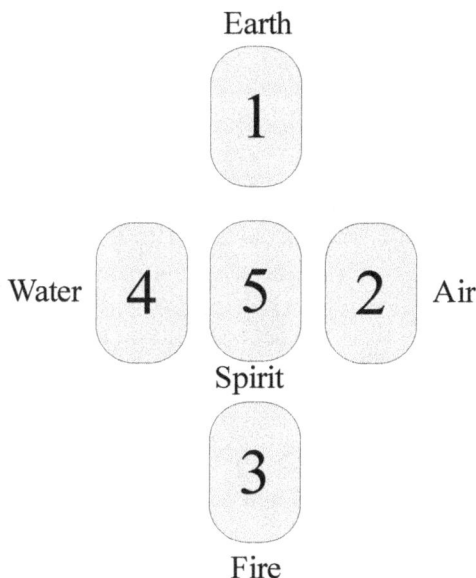

Earth

1

Water 4 5 2 Air

Spirit

3

Fire

Drawing 24

Sample Reading:

1. 5 of Stones
2. Ace of Swords
3. Ace of Wands
4. 2 of Cups
5. XV The Devil

I put cards in each of the positions in order, face up, until each was filled with a card relating to the element of that position. The cards indicated my two weakest areas at this time are my spiritual connection (The Devil) and my body (5 of Stones). Cards underneath may give a clue as to how I may seek balance.

64. Distance Healing
(a spread)

With this activity you can use the cards to help send positive healing energy to someone else. Please always ask the permission of that person before doing any work of this kind.

<u>Purpose</u>: To use the cards for sending positive healing energy.

<u>Procedure</u>:
1. Remove the four Aces and the Sun, Moon, and Star cards. Place in the pattern below.
2. Choose a card to represent the person to whom you are sending energy. Put that card in the middle of the spread.
3. Pull or choose a card that represents what that person needs. Put that card on top of the middle card horizontally.
4. Send the energy needed toward the person through concentrating your mind.

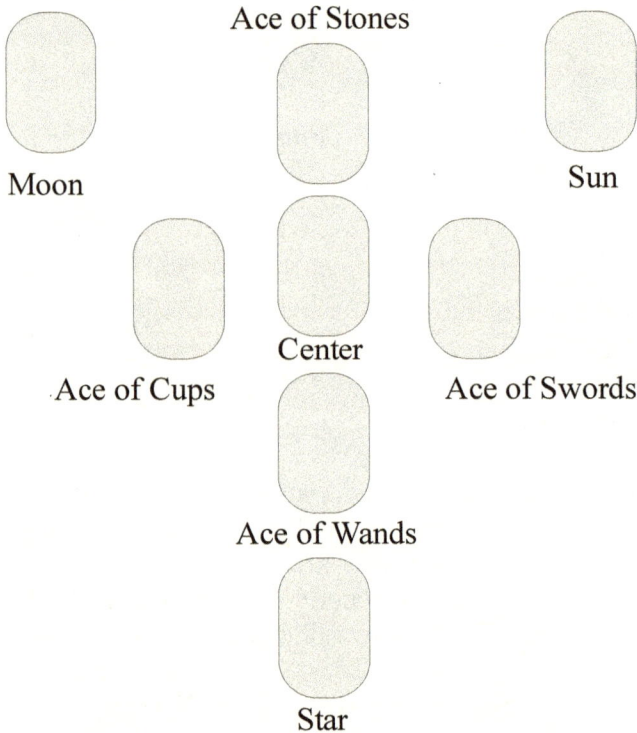

Ace of Stones

Moon   Sun

Center

Ace of Cups   Ace of Swords

Ace of Wands

Star

Drawing 25

65. Tarot Chi Kung
(a discovery)

Chi Kung and Tai Chi are Chinese ways of finding meditation, health, and peacefulness through slow body movements. Chi Kung tends to use less movements and is more focused on staying in one position while body motions are carried out. To take on this activity, you will need to separate out cards in your deck which have human figures. In the Quest deck, I found 27 cards that had human figures in different positions. These cards can be used to create a Tarot version of Chi Kung.

Purpose: To create a Chi Kung pattern.

Procedure:
1. Remove all cards with human figures.
2. Shuffle those cards and pull three (or more).
3. Lay those three in a horizontal line.
4. Create a movement pattern which slowly connects the shapes defines in the three cards. The movement should be done like a form of meditation.
5. Do the same pattern in each of the four directions.

Time and Space

66. Where Should I Go?
(a spread)

There comes a time when you know you need to go somewhere else but you do not know where that place may be. This activity can give you some ideas.

Purpose: To find out where you should go.

Procedure:
1. Pull four cards and place in the pattern below.
2. Determine where you should go from the cards.

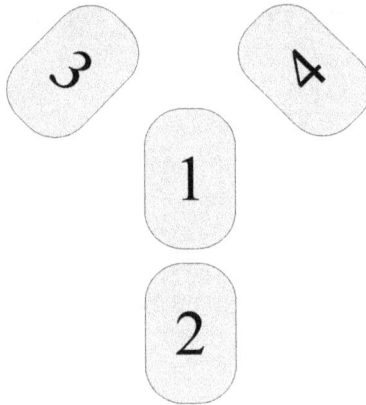

Drawing 26

Representations:
1. A clue as to where you should go.
2. What you will find when you get there.
3. Which direction you should go.
   a) Stones = North
   b) Swords = East
   c) Wands = South
   d) Cups = West
   e) Majors = nearby
4. How far you will need to travel.
   a) Ace = very near
   b) 10 = very far.

To get a better answer, use a map or globe and lay the number of cards next to each other on the map until you get to the chosen number. For example, if you pulled a 3 you would place a card on the map where you are now. Another card would be placed next to it in the chosen direction and a third card would indicate   the   general distance on the map.

Sample Reading:
1. Father of Stones
2. 0 The Fool
3. Son of Wands
4. 3 of Wands

The cards indicate that I should go to a place that will portray a sense of guardianship (Father of Stones). There I will find a new beginning (The Fool). To find this place I must travel South (Son of Wands) but I will not have to travel far (3 of Wands).

67. Karma and Destiny
(a spread)

Our present is defined by the past and also by the possibilities of the future. In this activity, you will explore your past by specifically looking at the karma or energy you have created in your life and the destiny that awaits you. Karma is a belief that everything we do impacts others both now and in the future. Most directly, our karma influences our present by requiring us to pay off our debts to the universe. If we cause suffering then we will experience suffering as well. Conversely, if we spread compassion we will also receive compassion. Instead of just observing the past and future, this activity also explores what can be done to make necessary adjustments.

Purpose: To observe your past karma and future destiny.

Procedure:
1. Pull seven cards and put into the spread below.
2. Compare the cards to their positions to get a reading.

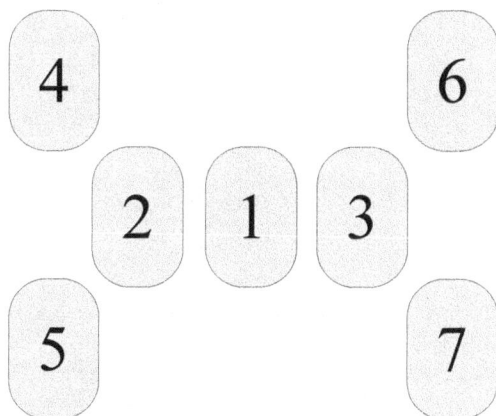

Drawing 27

Representations:
1. Your current state
2. Your past karma
3. Your possible future destiny
4. What you can do to balance your karma
5. The possible result of balancing your karma
6. What you can do to fulfill (or alter) your destiny
7. The possible result of fulfilling your destiny

Sample Reading:
1. XIII Death
2. III The Empress
3. 8 of Cups
4. 2 of Swords
5. Father of Swords
6. Ace of Cups
7. X The Wheel of Fortune

I am currently in a state of major change in my life (Death). My past karma involves not being able to balance the feminine (yin) aspects of myself (The Empress). This karma may lead to my possible destiny which is a possible failure or loss of spiritual alignment (8 of Cups). To avoid this possible result, I will need to balance my karma by seeking peace with my past attitudes about my feminine energies (2 of Swords). By doing so, I will better be able to take charge of my life (Father of Swords). I can alter the course of my destiny by being true to my inner emotions (Ace of Cups) rather than trying to suppress them. Doing so will lead to a major change that will be more successful than the path I am currently on (Wheel of Fortune).

68. Sacred Space
(a spread)

When I am traveling, I often cannot take a small altar with me as I go but I know that I can create a sacred space with just using a Tarot deck. The cards can help define a powerful space in which to worship, pray, and enact magick. This spread is not for divination; it is a pattern of cards that you can use to create your own portable ritual space. It is based on the numerological principle of creating a tetractys in a circle of 12. The tetractys or addition of 4 + 3 + 2 + 1 to get 10 was considered by the Pythagoreans to be a sacred representation of the basic elements of the universe created through geometric principles. Twelve symbolizes the zodiac which circles Earth and 12 is also the number of equally sized solid spheres that can surround a single sphere with all sides touching. Many religious practices understood the idea that 12 represented a complete encompassing whole while 13 represents the whole plus the center or leader. With these numerological principles, you can create a very powerful space using your cards. You can choose to use the entire Major Arcana to create a ritual space or just use a few of the cards to create a smaller or more portable altar.

<u>Purpose</u>: To create a portable ritual space or altar.

<u>Procedure</u>:
1. Remove the following cards from the deck:
   a) all aces
   b) The Emperor
   c) The Empress
   d) The Fool
   e) The Sun
   f) The Moon
   g) The Star
2. From the reminder of the deck, create your ritual space by placing any 12 cards face down in a circle.
3. Place the removed cards in the following spread.
4. Sit just behind the Center position in the circle and enact your ritual.

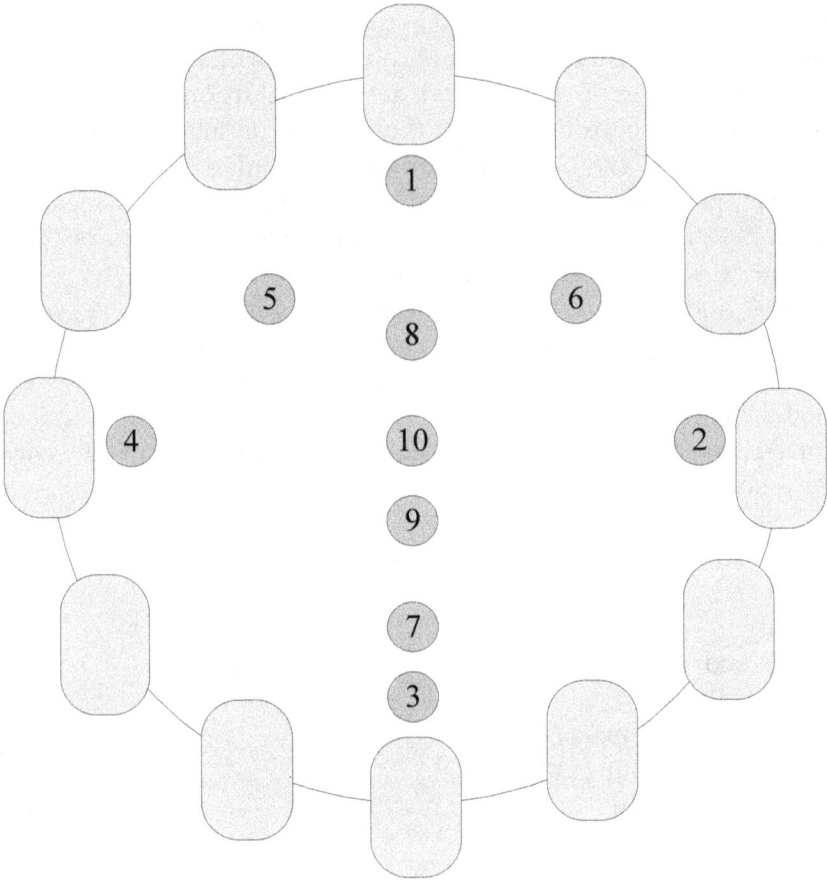

Drawing 28

Other Limitations

69. Practicing Restraint
(a spread)

If we cannot learn to restrain our desires, we can inadvertently hurt ourselves and others. There are times when we need to learn to practice restraint. This activity can help you find out where you need to limit yourself and how you can help yourself do that.

<u>Purpose</u>: To determine where you need to practice restraint.

Procedure:
1. Pull three cards and place in the following spread.
2. Determine where in your life you need restraint and how you will accomplish it.

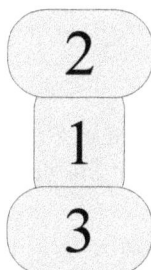

Drawing 29

Representations:
1. Where you need to apply restraint.
2. How to apply it externally.
3. How to apply it internally.

Sample Reading:
1. Son of Cups
2. 7 of Swords
3. 6 of Swords

I need to apply restraint in incessantly seeking spiritual truth (Son of Cups). I can apply that restraint externally by accepting the mystery that surrounds me while remembering that knowing all things about Spirit is impossible (7 of Swords). Internally, I can apply that restraint by understanding and being patient with my own spiritual sense of knowing (6 of Swords).

70. Applying Boundaries
(a spread)

This activity is, in a way, the opposite of the previous activity. Applying restraint is an internal limitation. Creating boundaries is a manner of setting external limitations. We all need to set boundaries in our lives. There are times when people "go too far" and cross the lines of personal respect and honor. We must create these boundaries within ourselves and make it clear to others when they have crossed them. Of course, we need to respect the boundaries of others as well.

<u>Purpose</u>: To determine where boundaries need to be set and how that can be done.

<u>Procedure</u>:
1. Pull three cards and place in the following spread.
2. Determine where in your life you need boundaries.

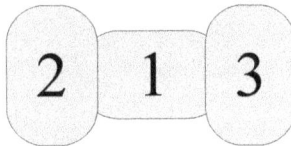

Drawing 30

<u>Representations</u>:
1. Where you need to set boundaries.
2. and
3. How to set those boundaries.

<u>Sample Reading</u>:
1. 4 of Stones
2. 8 of Swords
3. XVIII The Moon

    I need to set boundaries in my home and my work place (4 of Stones) by demanding that I be allowed to be visionary without disruption so that I can be more creative and productive (8 of Swords and The Moon).

Chapter 9

The Stars and Further Possibilities

Introduction

In this chapter, we will explore other possibilities for the Tarot. We will begin with some exercises for learning the cards themselves. These activities are good for both beginner and novice alike. Beginners and teachers of beginners can use these exercises to help their students become very familiar and comfortable with the cards themselves. This chapter also includes some of my favorite divination spreads that I have found useful in my time as a professional Tarot reader and, more recently, with my work in using the Tarot as a tool for advising and counseling.

Learning The Cards

71. Matching Qualities
(a discovery)

In this activity, you will seek out any two cards that have matching qualities between them. Every card has some interesting qualities to it especially within its artwork.

Purpose: To learn the Tarot through matching unique qualities between any two cards.

Procedure:

1. Pull any card.
2. Identify a quality of that card. The attribute can be anything within the artwork or it can be any aspect of the meaning or significance of the card. This quality should be something more than just the elemental suit or the number.
3. Choose another card that has that same or similar quality.

<u>Sample</u>:
Card pulled: 2 of Cups
Quality identified: the symbol of the joining of two symbolized by two rings.
Card chosen as a match: XX Aeon because of the joining of two forces symbolized by two roads that lead to the birth of a new child. (Several other cards could have been chosen as well.)

72. Quartets
(a discovery)

It can be helpful to compare the four cards of the same number or court figure in order to help you gain a deeper understanding of the meaning of that number or court character.

<u>Purpose</u>: To learn the Tarot through matching cards of the same number or court personality.

<u>Procedure:</u>
1. Find four cards of the same number or court personality (kings, queens, sons, daughters, etc.)
2. Compare the cards to find some similar meanings and symbols.

<u>Sample</u>:
Cards chosen: 2 of Stones, 2 of Swords, 2 of Wands, 2 of Cups.
Similarities: All the 2 cards seem to illustrate a dual nature in the reading of the cards in that all the art work shows both a joining and a separation. The number 2 in Tarot is both about the uniting of two but it is also about the change that occurs when two come together. At the same time, the 2 cards remind us that no two things completely merge into one and that all things retain some of their original

character even in the midst of transformation.

73. Identify The Personality
(a discovery)

In many divinatory readings, a center card is assigned the position of being the significator which is a card that is meant to represent the person seeking an answer through the cards. Usually, a person is identified first (the querent) and then a card is found to represent that person. In this activity, you will actually reverse that procedure.

Purpose: To learn the Tarot by determining personalities represented through any card.

Procedure:
1. Pull any card.
2. Determine the qualities of a person that card may represent.

Sample:
Card chosen: 9 of Wands
Personality: A highly energetic individual that seeks power and control. This person
can draw people together with his strong character and even make lasting relationships but his thirst for control can over power his better qualities and lead to difficult times.

74. The Formula
(a discovery)

This activity uses a common mathematical formula to create a way to find common ground between three different cards. It helps in practicing to identify three cards at a time while also looking for similarities between those cards.

Purpose: To learn the Tarot by comparing three cards.

Procedure:

1. Pull any three cards and set them in a horizontal spread naming them A, B, and C.
2. Identify the meanings of each.
3. Use the following formula to find deeper meanings to the cards: A is to B as B is to C.

Sample:
Cards chosen:
1. Daughter of Swords
2. V Heirophant
3. 5 of Wands

Comparison: The Daughter of Swords in the Quest deck is subtitled Confidence. The Hierophant is the teacher but is subtitled Tradition. Overconfidence in teaching leads to a staleness that can create a loss of innovation in instruction. An overuse of tradition without learning to accept innovation and change or without a continuing sense of excitement about a subject can lead to certain staleness in teaching (5 of Wands). Consequently, poor teaching fails to inspire students to learn. Therefore, overconfidence is to poor teaching as poor teaching is to stale learning.

75. What Card Am I?
(a game)

This activity is best done with a small group of people. It can played as a game by using all the Tarot cards to represent personalities or human characteristics. There are two ways to play: The first is to have people put a card on their forehead while others try to help each person figure out who they are. The second is to have people pull a card and look at it without revealing it to others and then have the group do an activity (like introduce each other). During the activity, people would act in the character of the card or possess a peculiar trait described by the card while others try to guess that card. The first game is described below.

Purpose: To learn the cards by identifying and portraying characteristics of that card.

Procedure:
1. Have everyone in the group pull a card without looking at it.
2. Everyone should place the card face out on their forehead.
3. People should try and guess the card that is on their forehead from the clues given by others in the group.
4. Play continues until all have guessed their own card.

Additional Rules:
Words that cannot be used are numbers, names of suits, name of the cards themselves, any other words already on the cards.

My Favorite Spreads

76. Shanddy's Pentagram Spread
(a spread)

During the time that I read Tarot professionally I tried a lot of different spreads to help people answer their questions. Certain spreads seemed to work well for certain situations and so I always had several possibilities available to me. Sometimes it helps to have one particular spread to which you consistently return as your default spread. I was familiar with the often used Celtic Cross Spread but found that it did not work as well for me as I hoped. Eventually, I created some of my own and this particular spread is the one to which I constantly turned and which proved to be most useful.

Purpose: To use as a spread for divination.

Procedure: Pull seven cards and place in the following spread.

Drawing 31

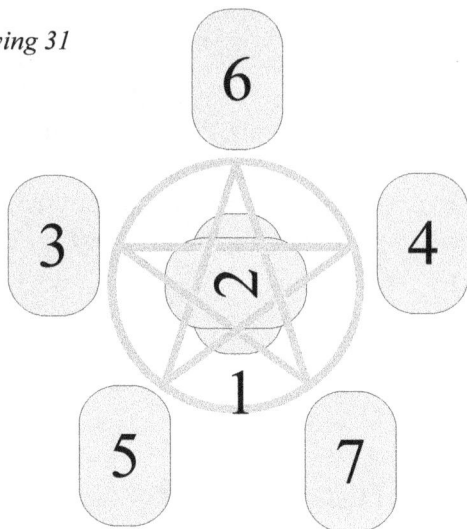

Representations:
1. (vertical card) Current situation or significator
2. (horizontal card) Block or interference
3. Past influence
4. Future probability
5. The key to change
6. Hopes and dreams for change
7. Future probability for change

Special Notes:
1. Card 2 acts as both a bridge between 3 and 4 and as a symbol of what might prevent one from reaching the hopes and dreams (6) or future probability (7).
2. Cards 1-4 describe the current line of possibilities. If the probability of card 4 is undesirable then 5 is a symbol of how one can seek a change.
3. Cards 5 -7 indicate a secondary line of possibilities if one incurs change. If 7 is desirable, 5 and 6 help indicate how to reach it. If 7 is undesirable, 5 and 6 indicate how to avoid it.

77. The Attainment Spread
(a spread)

People come to Tarot readings for some similar reasons. One of the things they often want to know is how to attain something they perceive that they need. This spread helps you determine how to identify and achieve a perceived need.

<u>Purpose</u>: To use as a divination spread for attaining a particular goal.

<u>Procedure</u>:
1. Pull or choose a card that represents your current situation on relation to your need.
2. Pull or choose a card that represents your need or desire.
3. Pull six additional cards.
4. Place the cards in the following spread pattern.
5. Interpret the cards according to their representations.

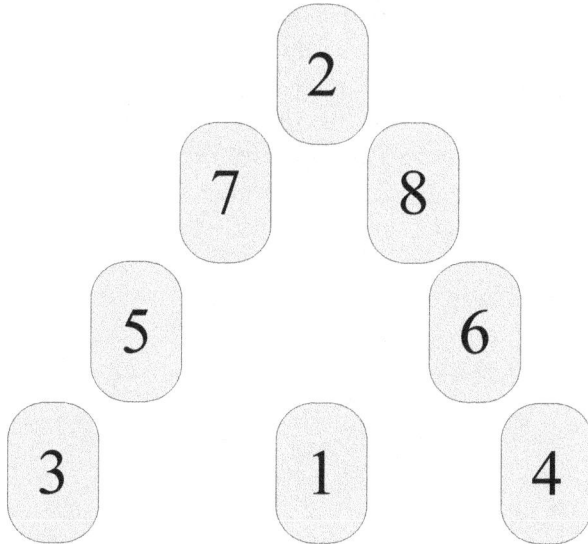

Drawing 32

<u>Representations</u>:
1. Your current state of need.
2. Your desired or perceived goal.

3. That which is driving your need.
4. What your need may fulfill in your life.
5. Something which is preventing you from attaining your goal.
6. Something which may help you in your goal.
7. How to proceed.
8. Where to seek guidance.

Sample Reading:
1. Ace of Wands
2. 2 of Wands
3. Son of Swords
4. 9 of Stones
5. V Hierophant
6. Ace of Cups
7. 5 of Swords
8. 4 of Swords

I am currently feeling emotionally strong and passionate (Ace of Wands) but seek an emotional change (2 of Wands). Let us say that I desire to find more friends. What is driving my need is a desire to connect with others intellectually (Son of Swords). Fulfilling that need may help to create for me a sense of material security or a stronger sense of belonging in my community (9 of Stones). What is preventing me from my goal is being able to break out of my current work and life routine so that I may seek groups of people who enjoy learning together (V Hierophant). Focusing on the joy I find when conversing with others may help me attain my goal (Ace of Cups). I need to proceed by ending my current way of thinking (5 of Swords). I can seek guidance with those who seek peace of mind (4 of Swords).

78. The Crossroads Spread
(a spread)

Many people also seek answers from the cards to help them make decisions. If there is a tough choice to be made between two options, this spread can help someone observe the possible consequences of each decision.

<u>Purpose</u>: To use as a divination spread in making a decision.

<u>Procedure</u>:
1. Pull or choose a card to represent where you are presently in your decision.
2. Pull an additional eight cards and place in the following pattern.

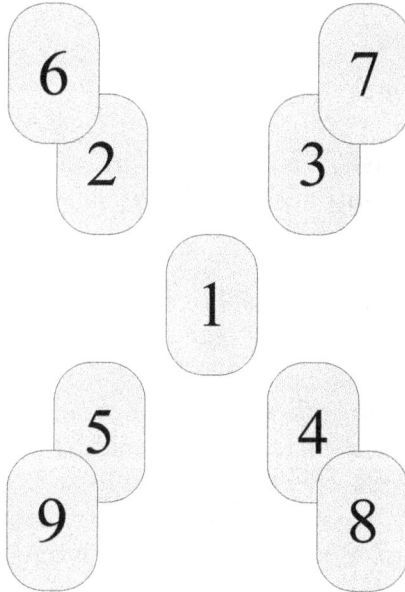

Drawing 33

<u>Representations</u>:
1. Where you are currently in your decision.
2. A major factor influencing card 6.
3. A major factor influencing card 7.
4. A major factor influencing card 8.
5. A major factor influencing card 9.
6. External effect of first choice or stasis (how it will affect others).
7. External effect of second choice or change.
8. Internal effect of first choice or stasis (how it will affect you).
9. Internal effect of second choice or change.

Sample Reading:
1. IV The Emperor
2. XX Aeon
3. Son of Swords
4. Father of Wands
5. Mother of Wands
6. Father of Swords
7. 2 of Wands
8. 3 of Wands
9. XV The Devil

As I write this, it is Saturday morning and I must decide whether or not to continue writing or take a break. I chose the Emperor as the significator because, as the earthly male figure, he likes to eat and enjoy himself. Card 6 tells me that if I continue to write (choose stasis), the effect on others is that I will help create a new pathway of thought (Father of Swords) which is influenced by the need to create new things (Aeon). The external effect of my taking a break is that I will help others experience an emotional change (my wife will love the fact that I will spend some time to enjoy her company) and that this effect will be influenced by my desire to be considerate about not working through the morning (Son of Swords). The internal effect of not changing the current situation will be to enjoy the creativity of writing (3 of Wands) influenced by my desire to express what I have learned (Father of Wands). The internal effect of choosing to take a break is that I will be tempted to eat and not want to return to the writing. This is influenced by the emotional pleasure I receive from indulging myself (Mother of Wands). It seems that I better continue to write for a while longer which is all right for now because my wife is still sleeping.

Appendix 1

Tarot Games

esides being a great system of divination, the Tarot cards can also be used to play games. Admit it, you have more than one Tarot deck lying around the house. At least one of those decks is probably considered old and useless. Why not use it to play some games and have some fun? In this section, I will offer 14 different and original (except for the classic Tarot) games that can be played with a Tarot deck.

Although many of these games have been tested out by several people you should feel free to alter the rules to make any game more fun or challenging as your play group sees fit.

1. Classic Tarot

Some historians believe that the Tarot was originally used for playing games and one game may even have been called Tarot or Tarocchi which was very similar to today's game of Bridge. In this game, I have simplified the rules for the classical Tarot game to make it easy to play. You will need to determine the rank of the Court cards.

Number of Players: 4

Equipment:
1. 1 Tarot deck
2. paper and pencil for scoring

Objective: To complete a bid or prevent others from completing a bid.

Procedure:

1. All the cards are passed out to all the players with a fifth (dummy) hand also included. The dummy hand cards are left face down on the table.
2. Players call out bids. The one calling the highest bid is called the "Taker." The other three players compete against the Taker to prevent him or her from completing the bid.
   a) If the Taker fulfills the bid or more, the Taker counts the points.
   b) If not, all the other players count their points.
3. The winner is the first one to 300 points.

Additional Rules:
1. Players lead by suits and the highest card in a suit takes the trick.
2. Major Arcana cards are trump.
3. Trumps can only be played when no cards in a suit are available or when they are led.
4. Aces are high (they take Court cards).
5. Zero cards can be played anytime and trump everything. (The Void card can be a zero card)

Card Points:
1. Zero cards (Fool, Multiverse, Void) = 5 points
2. Aces, X Wheel of Fortune, and XXI The Universe = 4 points
3. Mothers and Fathers = 3 points
4. Daughters and Sons = 2 points
5. All other cards = 1 point

Sample Play:
Cards are dealt out to the five players plus the "Dummy." Player 1 bids 3. Player 2 bids 4. Player 3 bids 2 as does Player 4. Player 2 is the Taker. Player 2 lays down an Ace of Cups. All players must lead Cups if they have them. All follow suit. Game continues until all cards are played and the players count their points.

2. Tahtzee (Tarot Yahtzee)

Yahtzee is a popular dice game that can be played by one or

more people scoring points. This version, of course, uses Tarot cards so I have decided to call it Tahtzee.

<u>Number of Players</u>: 1 or more

<u>Equipment</u>:
1. 1 Tarot deck
2. copies of scoring sheets

<u>Objective</u>: To score as many points as possible in one round.

<u>Procedure</u>:
Shuffle the deck and lay down five cards. You may remove any number of the five cards and replace them with cards on top of the deck. The cards may then be replaced a third time. After the third time, score the result in the score box. When all boxes are filled, the round is over and points should be calculated. A score box must be filled each time. If your result does not match exactly the description of the category, a zero must be entered into one of the other score boxes.

Table X.1 Tahtzee Scoring Form

Score Box	Points	Your score	max
MINORS			
Aces	1 each		4
Twos	2 each		8
Threes	3 each		12
Fours	4 each		16
Fives	5 each		20
Sixes	6 each		24
SUITS			
Stones	add numbers		50
Swords	add numbers		50
Wands	add numbers		50
Cups	add numbers		50
COURTS	10		50
COMBINATIONS			
3 of a kind	5		5
4 of a kind	10		10
Short Stack (7,8,9,10)	20		20
Family (Father, Mother, Daugher, Son)	25 per suit		100
MAJORS			
Elemental (one Minor of each suit plus one Major)	25		25
Foundation (four Majors)	Add numbers		78
Straight (ANY five numbers in order)	50		50
1st Tahtzee (all Majors)	Add numbers		95
2nd Tahtzee	Add numbers		95

Score Box	Points	Your score	max
3rd Tahtzee	Add numbers		95
TOTALS			817

Sample Play:

    I turn over five cards: XVII The Star, 5 of Stones, 5 of Swords, XXI The Universe, and the Ace of Stones. I decide to play for the fives and remove all cards except the two 5 cards. I take three more cards and get: 8 of Stones, Mother of Swords, and Mother of Wands. No help there. I decide to try again and get: Son of Swords, XI Justice, and XVIII The Moon. I score the two 5 cards in the Fives category for 10 points.

3. Tarot Strategy

    This game combines chess with other strategy games. The cards create a chance to incorporate both chance and strategy into one game.

Number of Players: 2-4

Equipment:
1. one deck for each player.
2. 8x8 playing board with squares large enough to hold the Tarot cards.

Objective: To capture the other team's Emperor and Empress cards.

Procedure:
1. Lay out an 8x8 board. Play actually begins off the board.
2. Players shuffle their decks and then set eight cards face down in front of their place on the board. There can be one player on each side of the board. If there are only two players, they should play opposite each other.
3. For each round a player has three choices:
    a) move a card onto the board;
    b) move forward; or

c) attack.

4. One card from the row in front of the board can be moved face up onto its corresponding space on the board if there is an exposed space on that row. After doing so, another card from the player's deck is placed face down in the empty space in front of the board. Once on the board, a card can be moved forward or attack another card according to the movement and attack chart below. You cannot both move to an empty space and attack but you can move to an occupied space to attack. In attacking, higher numbers beat out lower numbers except for the Ace which is high.

5. Players who lose both their Emperor and Empress cards are out of the game. The winner is the last player remaining.

Table X.2 Tarot Strategy Game Attack and Movement Chart

Card	Movement	Attack	Defeats
all Minor Arcana cards	forward one space	forward only	lower Minors
all Court cards	forward any direction	forward and diagonal	all Minors adults defeat children
all Major Arcana	one space any direction	any direction	all other cards and lower Majors
Families	none	any direction one space	any card but Death or the Devil

Additional Rules:
Some cards have special privileges:

1. The Fool can jump to ANY open space on the board.
2. The Magician and the High Priestess can move any number of consecutive open spaces.
3. 0 cards can take any other cards.
4. The Void card can be placed ONCE anywhere on the board where it will remain unmoved for the remainder of the game.
5. Any Mother, Father, Daughter, and Son can be stacked

together in one space in any desired order. When this is done, the stack is called a family. Families can only be defeated by the Death or Devil cards. Once completed, a family cannot move except to attack one space in any direction. Families can be broken up at any time. An incomplete family has the characteristics of its top card. When attacked, incomplete families only lose the top card in the stack. The attacking card will remain on the incomplete stack and be unable to move until removed by attack from another card.

6. Cards placed on an opposing person's front row block that person from adding a new card to the board.

4. Cosmic Twenty-One

Similar to Blackjack, in this game players try to make a total of 21 points per round without going over 21. The addition of Major Arcana cards creates some new and interesting twists, however.

<u>Number of Players</u>: 2 – 8

<u>Equipment</u>: 1 Tarot deck

<u>Objective</u>: To make 21 points without going over to reach a total of 300.

<u>Procedure</u>:
1. Players start with one card face down. Players can then ask the dealer for another card face up in order to get as close to 21 points without going over.
2. Players can continue to ask for additional face up cards until they are ready to play. All numbers on all cards are counted. Court cards count as 10 points. Void cards are a choice of 0 or 10.
3. The winner of each round scores points made. Other players who do not go over 21 points may also score points.
4. The person with the greatest number of points without going over 21 gets 10 additional points.
5. Game ends at 300 points.

Additional Rules:
1. The Universe XXI card is an instant winner regardless of other cards present and its holder gets 21 points regardless of who wins the round.
2. Holders of the Sun, Moon, and Star cards get an additional 10 points each regardless of winner.
3. Players with more than five cards that do not go over 21 get 5 additional points regardless of winner.

5. The Great Pyramid

The idea for this game came from the Chinese game called Mah-Johng. It can be played as a one player solitaire game or it can be altered slightly for play with two or four persons. You will need exactly 78 cards for this game so remove any extras such as the Void or Multiverse cards.

Number of Players: 1, 2, or 4

Equipment: One Tarot Deck

Objective:
For one player: to remove all the cards from the table.
For two or four players: to be the person with the most matches or to be the first to run out of cards completely.

Procedure:
Lay out the cards in the following manner:
1. Make four piles of six cards each, face down.
2. Create a pyramid of the remaining cards face down by making a 5x5 grid. On top of those cards make a 4x4 grid by placing cards on the inside corners of the 5x5 grid.

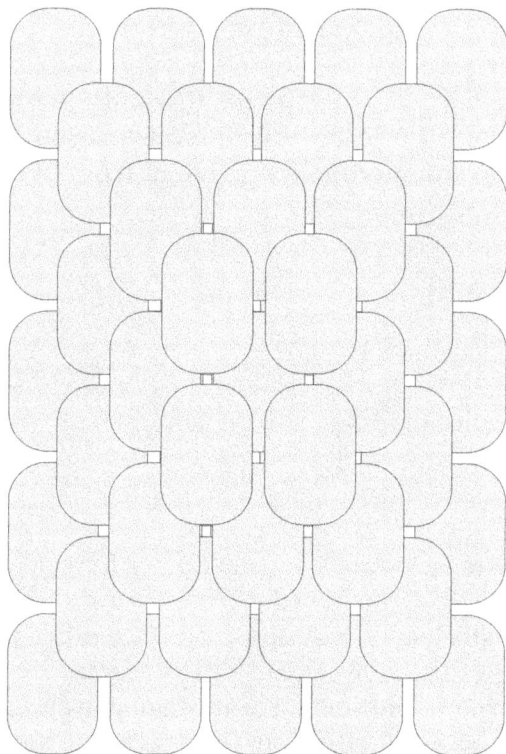

Drawing 34

3. Next make a 3x3 grid and then a 2x2 grid on top.
4. For one player: place the four stacks in front of you and turn them over. For two players: two stacks are placed in front of each player and are turned face up. Only cards which are not covered may be turned over. One card only can be turned over each round.
5. Cards are turned over one at a time and matched with other exposed cards. Matching cards are:
   a) Minor Arcana cards with the same number
   b) Court cards of the same value (Mother matches Mother, etc.)
   c) all Major Arcana cards match each other.

Additional Rules:
For two or four players: If a match is made, that player can continue to match any remaining exposed cards.

6. At The Races

This is a fairly simple game that may be a lot of fun for children (of all ages). For each player, remove a suit of Minor Arcana cards and set them up into one long row in front of you. This will be your race track.

Number of Players: 2-4

Equipment: One Tarot deck.

Objective: To be the first one whose horse (Ace) reaches the end of the track (beyond the 10 card).

Procedure:
1. Create your race track by making a long row of one suit of Minor Arcana cards in order from 2 - 10.
2. Place the stack of remaining cards face down in the middle.
3. Each person turns over one card at a time.
4. If the card is a Major Arcana, that player moves their horse (Ace) one space further on the track. If the card is a Court card, the player must move the player whose Ace is the same suit of the Court card up one space.

Additional Rules:
1. If the Court card matches the suit of the player, move 2 spaces forward.

Special Cards:
1. Zero, Void, and XXI cards move two spaces forward.
2. Devil - move anyone one space backward.
3. Death - lose a turn.

7. Squad Attack

This is a fairly simple game to learn but can involve quite a bit of strategy as you must decide when to attack and when to surrender in hopes of getting better cards.

<u>Number of Players</u>: 2 - 8 (more players may involve two rounds of play)

<u>Equipment</u>: One Tarot deck

<u>Objective</u>: To collect the most cards through winning card battles.

<u>Procedure</u>:
1. Deal each player five cards which they will hold in front of them.
2. The first person puts down their Attack according to the rules below and others must put in cards to either Surrender or try to beat the attack. An Attack can be any number of cards. However, a player must put down cards in pairs or in particular combinations.
3. Unless the player does not have 2 of a kind, only then can one card be played. Players must put down at least one card in every round. Only one card can be played unless it is in combination with others.
4. The person whose card combination is highest takes all the cards. The following combinations are possible in order from lowest to highest:
   a) two of a kind (by numbers not suit):
      • Minor Arcana cards with same number
      • similar Court cards
      • any two Major Arcanas
   b) three of a kind
   c) four of a kind
   d) five of a kind (five Majors)
   e) A squad (one Minor of each suit and one Court card of any suit)
5. Except for the special cards and combinations, Major Arcana cards take Court cards and Minor Arcana cards and Court cards take Minor Arcana cards.
6. After playing a round, the winner places the cards off to the side and all players take cards to fill out their five card hand.
7. Play begins with the next player to the left of the last player..

Play continues until all cards are used.

Additional Rules:
1.   If two hands are the same kind (i.e. two people with fours of a kind) the highest number takes the trick.
2.   The Devil card takes all tricks.
3.   Aces are counted as 1 unless all four are collected in which case they are all higher than 10s.

8. Dungeon

This game is a very simplified version of the many famous dungeon type games. It can be played as a one player game or with multiple players. You will need a large playing space or you can use graph paper to mark out your progress through the dungeon that you will create along the way. You begin at the entrance to a strange dark cavern. Before beginning, you will need to decide where the four directions are in your playing space. You will begin by creating a character.

Number of Players: 1 – 4

Equipment:
1.   One or more Tarot decks
2.   graph paper
3.   paper and pencil

Objective: To be the first (or only) one to get into the dungeon, find 300 Gold Points and get back out alive.

Procedure:
1. Creating the Character: (write these on a sheet of paper)
    a) Name (pick a name)
    b) L = level (start at 1)
        • the player can move to the next level by reaching 10 points x the current level number
        • i.e. it takes 20 XP to go to level 2 and 30 XP to reach level 3,etc.

c) XP = experience points (pick a Minor Arcana card for beginning amount)

d) GP = gold points (start at 0)

e) S = strength (start at 50, increase by 10 points for each level and with specials)

f) HP = hit points (pull two Minor Arcana cards and multiply them together for the beginning amount)

2. Exploring the Dungeon

a) Mark the space on your graph where you or your group will begin so that you will know where to end as well.

b) Place the deck face down and pick the top card.

c) Play according to the following cards:

- Any Stones card - Create spaces and/or move your player North by the number on the card.
- Any Swords card - Create spaces and/or move your player East by the number on the card.
- Any Wands card - Create spaces and/or move your player South by the number on the card.
- Any Cups card - Create spaces and/or move your player West by the number on the card.

d) Court cards (Helpers)

- Father = 10 GP or purchase 1 strength at 50 GP.
- Mother = 10 GP or purchase 1 XP at 50 GP.
- Daughter and Son = 5 GP.

e) Majors (obstacles) engage in battle or receive Special

f) Spaces already created can be moved onto.

g) Once you have found 300 GP, return to Start to win.

3. Battling Demons

a) When a Major Arcana card is encountered in the dungeon, a battle must ensue between you and the enemy unless the enemy's card has a special ability. Pull the number of cards equal to your Strength level. Add up the total number of any cards with numbers (including Majors) with any numbers on the original card. The total is your Attack Points (AP). Court cards add 1x level AP. AP of the Major Arcana card is the strength level of the card times your current level.

- Determining the AP:
  - Major Arcana = _____
  - Court cards   = _____
  - other Minor = _____
  - total   = _____

b) To determine the enemy's AP, pull the number of cards equal to the enemy's Strength level and add in the same numbers as you did for your AP.

c) If you win the battle (your AP is higher than the card's AP) add the following to your character:
- The enemy's Experience Points (XP) to your XP.
- The enemy's Hit Points (HP) to your HP.
- The enemy's Gold Points (GP) to your GP.

d) If you lose, subtract the card's HP from your HP. If your HP goes below 0 then you have lost your life and the game. The following is the table of Major Arcana cards and their points and specials.

Table X.3 Dungeon Game Points

HP and XP	Card	GP and Strength	Special
0	The Fool	1 x level	
-	The Magician	no battle	increase your strength by 1
II	The High Priestess	1 x level	
III	The Empress	1 x level	
IV	The Emperor	1 x level	
V	Hierophant	1 x level	
VI	The Lovers	1 x level	
-	Chariot	no battle	move up to 5 spaces in any direction
VIII	Strength	1 x level	increase your strength by 1
IX	The Hermit	1 x level	
X	The Wheel of Fortune	2 x level	
XI	Justice	2 x level	
XII	The Hanged Man	2 x level	
XIII	Death	2 x level	
XIV	Alchemy	2 x level	
XV	The Devil	3 x level	if he wins, he steals 10 x level GP
-	The Tower	no battle	road block (cannot go any further)
XVII	The Star	3 x level	
XVIII	The Moon	3 x level	
XIX	The Sun	3 x level	
XX	Aeon	4 x level	
XXI	The Universe	4 x level	
0	The Multiverse	4 x level	no battle, increase XP by 1
25	blank card	5 x level	no battle, increase strength and XP by 1

Additional Rules:
1. Tunnels can be built between dungeon passages by paying 25 GP for each space between entrances.

Rules for multiple players:
1. Multiple players can race each other and attack each other.
2. Each player creates their own spaces within the dungeon.
3. Players winning an attack against another player take that player's:
   a) GP, 1 x level HP and 1 x level XP.

Special Cards:
1. Aces allow you to go in any direction with the next card.
2. The playing deck must be reshuffled each time an Ace is turned over during play.

9. Tarot Bowling

I remember going bowling with my friends as a kid and I remember how terrible I was at it. I think I threw more bowling balls in the gutter and in other people's lanes than I did in my own but I always had a good time. Here is a Tarot version of the game of bowling I created so that I would not hurt anyone. This is one of few games in which getting Major Arcana cards is a disadvantage.

Number of Players: any number

Equipment: One Tarot deck

Objective: To score the most points in 10 frames

Procedure:
For each player, do the following:
1. Shuffle the deck and place 10 cards face down in the typical bowling pin pattern. These will be referred to as the "pins."

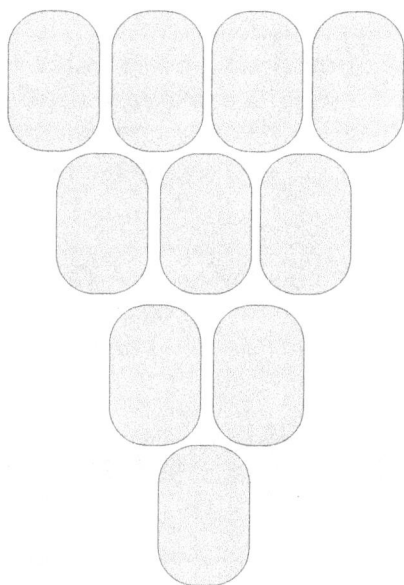

Drawing 35

2. Flip over the next card from the deck (face up).
   a) If the card is a Minor, choose that number of pins to turn over.
   b) If the card is a Court, mark a "spare" (/) in the scoring box.
   c) If the card is a Major Arcana, it is a "gutter ball" and no cards are turned over.
3. Count the number of face up cards which are Courts and Minors and enter this number in the left hand corner of the scoring box.
4. Replace any Major Arcana pins which are face up with new face down cards.
5. Flip over a second card from the deck.
   a) If the card is a Minor, choose that number of remaining face down pins to turn over.
   b) If the card is a Court, and the first card was also a Court, mark a "strike" (X) in the scoring box, otherwise, flip over all remaining face down pins.
   c) If the card is a Major Arcana, mark a zero in the scoring box.
6. Count the number of face up cards which are Courts and

Minors and enter this number in the right hand corner of the scoring box. Add the total number in the scoring box.
7. As in regular bowling, a strike in the 10th frame allows you to try for up to two more strikes.
8. Add up the scores after 10 completed frames.

Additional Rules:
1. A spare counts 10 plus the total of the number in the previous left hand box.
2. A strike counts 10 plus the total of the previous frame.

Table X. 4 Bowling Game Scoring Box

Frame	1	2	3	4	5	6	7	8	9	10	Total
Player 1	☐☐	☐☐	☐☐	☐☐	☐☐	☐☐	☐☐	☐☐	☐☐		
Player 2	☐☐	☐☐	☐☐	☐☐	☐☐	☐☐	☐☐	☐☐	☐☐		
Player 3	☐☐	☐☐	☐☐	☐☐	☐☐	☐☐	☐☐	☐☐	☐☐		
Player 4	☐☐	☐☐	☐☐	☐☐	☐☐	☐☐	☐☐	☐☐	☐☐		

Sample Play:
        I begin frame one by setting out 10 cards face down in the pins pattern. I turn over the next card in the deck and get the 5 of Wands. This allows me to turn over 5 "pins." When I do, I get three Major Arcana cards, 1 Court card, and 1 Minor Arcana card. I mark 2 in the left hand scoring box. I discard the 3 Majors and leave the Court and the Minor cards on the table. I replace the discarded 3 Majors with 3 new face down cards. I flip over the next card in the deck and get the Daughter of Stones. This allows me to turn over all remaining pins. I turn over 5 Majors, 1 Minor and 2 Court cards. I mark 2 in the right hand scoring box which gives me a total of 5.

10. Out!

This is a Tarot version of the popular form of those Crazy Eight games. People of all ages like these kinds of games.

<u>Number of Players</u>: 2 – 8

<u>Equipment</u>: One Tarot deck

<u>Objective</u>: To be the first person to get rid of their cards.

<u>Procedure</u>:
1. Begin with 7 cards passed out to each player.
2. First player puts down a card.
3. Next player can put a card on top of that card if it is a Minor or Court card that matches the suit or number.
4. Major Arcana cards match other Majors.
5. If none of the cards in a player's hand can be matched, the player picks up one card.
6. The player who matches the last card puts down that card and yells "Out!"

<u>Additional Rules:</u>
1. Cards picked up cannot be played in the same round.

<u>Special Cards:</u> The following table lists the special cards for play.

Table X.5 Out! Game Special Cards

Card	Special
0 The Fool	Nothing
I The Magician	Next player draws one card
II The High Priestess	Next player draws two cards
III The Empress	Next player draws three cards
IV The Emperor	Next player draws 4 cards
V Hierophant	Play 2 cards of same suit
VI The Lovers	Player puts down an additional card
VII Chariot	Skip next two players
VIII Strength	No! card: avoid any future penalties
IX The Hermit	Player gives one card to the next player
X The Wheel of Fortune	Direction of play is reversed
XI Justice	Player gives one card to another player
XII The Hanged Man	Direction of play is reversed
XIII Death	Skip next player
XIV Alchemy	Double the effect of previously played card to next player.
XV The Devil	Player MAY switch hands with another player
XVI The Tower	All other players draw 1 card
XVII The Star	Wild card! Call out a suit
XVIII The Moon	Wild card! Call out a suit
XIX The Sun	Wild card! Call out a suit
XX Aeon	Free card! Avoid any penalties and call a suit
XXI The Universe	Free card! Avoid any penalties and call a suit
0 The Multiverse	Free card! Avoid any penalties and call a suit
blank card	Free card! Avoid any penalties and call a suit

11. Tarot Baseball

I have to admit that I love baseball so I just had to come up with a Tarot version of baseball and here it is. To play, separate your deck into a stack of Major Arcana, a stack of Minor Arcana, and a stack of Court cards. There are four possible teams that can play: the Stones, the Swords, the Wands, and the Cups. I can just imagine the jerseys now!

Number of Players: 2

Equipment:
1. 1 Tarot deck
2. pencil and paper

Objective: To make the most points in 9 innings or rounds with your team.

Preparation:

Remove any extra Major Arcana cards from the deck. Each player should choose one suit as his or her team and take out the four Major Arcana cards of that suit. Set up the playing field by using four Court cards not chosen as a team to create the baseball diamond. Shuffle the Major Arcana cards and put them in a stack face down in the middle of the diamond (the pitcher's mound). Shuffle the Minor cards and place them face down on the table. Each player is given five cards from the Minor pile which they keep in their hands. Players decide who goes first and puts their team "on deck" or in a pile near the home plate of the diamond. The person who goes first is the batter while the other is the pitcher.

Procedure:
1. The batter and the pitcher begin by laying down one of the cards in their hands. The cards represent something for each player (see below).
2. The pitcher has the choice of either pitching a strike or a ball.
3. The hitter has the choice of swinging or not swinging at a pitch.

4. These choices are made depending on the number of the card:
   a) Pitcher
      - Ace to Five = ball
      - Six to Ten = strike
   b) Batter
      - Ace to Five = no swing
      - Six to Ten = swing
5. The combinations create four possible results:

	Ball	Strike
No swing	Ball	Strike
Swing	Strike	Hit

6. When the players have lain down their cards, they determine the outcome according to the chart. Balls and strikes should be recorded as usual. Four balls is a walk and three balls is an out. Results of balls, strikes, and points should be recorded on a piece of paper. After the result is recorded, the players take another card to maintain five in their hands and begin again until the half inning is over. After three outs, players trade roles: the batter becomes the pitcher and vice versa.
7. If a hit is made, one of the Major Arcana cards are turned over and the results table is read. If a player gets a hit and advances to a base, one of the team cards is placed on the base card.
8. A point a is scored for each player that makes it around to all bases to the home plate. The Major Arcana cards should be re-shuffled after one card has been turned over. After each player has been both pitcher and batter, the inning is over.
9. Players continue until nine innings are completed.

Table X.6 Baseball Game Hit Chart

Card	Correspondence
0 The Fool	sacrifice
I The Magician	pop fly - out
II The High Priestess	pop fly - out
III The Empress	pop fly - out
IV The Emperor	foul
V Hierophant	foul
VI The Lovers	foul
VII Chariot	foul
VIII Strength	stolen base
IX The Hermit	stolen base
X The Wheel of Fortune	base hit
XI Justice	base hit
XII The Hanged Man	base hit
XIII Death	base hit
XIV Alchemy	base hit
XV The Devil	base hit
XVI The Tower	double
XVII The Star	double
XVIII The Moon	double
XIX The Sun	triple
XX Aeon	triple
XXI The Universe	home run
0 The Multiverse	(removed)
blank card	(removed)

12. Bluff

<u>Number of Players</u>: 2 – 8

<u>Equipment</u>: One Tarot deck

<u>Objective</u>: To be the first player to lay down seven cards.

<u>Procedure</u>:

1. The deck is shuffled and placed down on the table. Each player takes a turn by picking the top card from the deck and looking at it.
2. The player then has three choices:
   a) discard the card.
   b) place the card on the table.
   c) challenge another player (if the player has cards on the table).
3. If the card is discarded, the player's turn is over. If the card is placed on the table, it is open to future challenge by any players who have a card on the table. If a player has a card on the table, that player can challenge another player with at least one card on the table.
4. To challenge, the player accuses another player. That player must show the last card put down. If that player's card is a Major card, that player keeps the card and the challenger must remove one of his or her cards from the table. If the challenged player's card is not a Major card, it must be removed.
5. Additional cards put on the table should slightly overlap previous cards to show which card was the last one played. After six cards have been lain on the table, a player wins by placing a seventh card on the stack which must be a Major card.

<u>Additional Rules:</u>
Only top cards can be challenged.

13. Tarot Golf

Here's a card version of the popular game of golf. With this version, you do not have to go outside and wear those strange colored pants.

Number of Players: 1 – 8

Equipment:
1. One Tarot deck
2. Pencil and paper for scoring

Objective: To have the lowest score at the end of nine "holes."

Procedure:
1. Separate your Major cards out of the deck. Shuffle them and place nine in the center of the table, face down. These will be the nine "holes."
2. Turn the top Major card over to begin the first "hole." Players must use the cards in their hands to match the number shown on the Major card. The first player begins by laying down as many cards that add up or come close to the total number on the Major card without going over.
3. If the player does not match the number exactly, then a stroke is counted for the player. That player then replaces the number of cards lain down to maintain three cards in their hand at all times.
4. The next player then makes the same attempt. If the player can match the number on the first try, a "hole in one" is called out. For each hole, players can go no more than 6 rounds.
5. If, after six rounds, the player has still not made the total then 6 strokes is counted against the player, play for that hole stops, and the next Major card is revealed for the next hole.
6. At the end of nine holes, players count their totals with the lowest score winning. Tied players may play an additional hole as a tie-breaker.

Special Cards:
 1. Court cards can count as either ones or tens - player's choice.
 2. 0 and Void cards count as 25.
 3. I The Magician - the last player to make a "hole in one" can call the total otherwise, the total is 25.
 4. II High Priestess - Water Trap. Only Cups cards can be used for the total.
 5. III Empress - Sand Trap. Only Stones can be used for the total.
 6. IV Emperor - High Winds. Only Swords can be used for the total.
 7. V Hierophant - Fire Trap. Only Wands can be used for the total.

14. Tarot Towers

This is a wild, fast paced game simply because players do not take turns. Instead, everyone plays all at once. Players try to make stacks of four cards called Tarot Towers. You may want to use a very old deck for this game as the cards can get a little bent with all the grabbing going on.

Number of Players: 2 – 8

Equipment: One Tarot deck

Objective: To get as many points from Towers built before the game ends.

Procedure:
 1. Deal five cards to each player.
 2. Place four cards on the table face up leaving room for the deck to go in the middle of them. Place the deck in the middle of play where everyone can easily reach it. Once the deck is put on the table, play begins.
 3. Players begin taking cards. Players may never have more than five cards in their hand at any time. Cards may be taken from the deck or from the four cards on the table. When a card is taken from the table, the player must replace the taken card

with one from his or her hand. When taking a card from the deck, the player must also discard to one of the four piles around the deck. Only the top card of each discard pile can be taken.

4. A Tarot Tower is created by having four cards all of the same suit with one Major card. Once a Tower is built the player calls out "Tower" and it is laid down face down in a pile in front of the player and new cards are taken from the deck. Play ends when all cards are taken from the deck or when all players are unable to continue.

5. Players look at their Towers and count points from the number on the Major card associated with each stack. Player with the highest points wins.

Additional Rules:
1. Towers that have four cards of the same number and suit count double points.
2. A Tower with a four card straight (i.e. Ace, 2, 3 4) counts double.
3. A four card straight of the same suit counts triple.
4. Players that do not call out "Tower" when completing a Tower may have their Tower stolen.

Special Cards:
1. O and void cards are wild.
2. The Tower card is an automatic Tarot Tower of its own.

Appendix 2

List of Activities

he following is a complete list of all the activities in the book.

Activity Index

Illustration Index

Drawing Index

Activity Index

Correspondences

This text contains a great many Tarot correspondences. I have included several additional useful correspondences at the end of this index.

Table X.9 Time Correspondences

Card	Correspondence
Minors	days from now
Majors	weeks from now
Courts:	
Daughter	3 months
Son	6 months
Mother	9 months
Father	12 months

Table X.10 *Virtue Correspondences*

Card	Correspondence
0 The Fool	humility
I The Magician	patience
II The High Priestess	devotion
III The Empress	sympathy
IV The Emperor	courage, dignity
V Hierophant	learning
VI The Lovers	unselfishness
VII Chariot	perseverance
VIII Strength	understanding
IX The Hermit	introspection
X The Wheel of Fortune	flexibility
XI Justice	loyalty
XII The Hanged Man	modesty, sacrifice
XIII Death	caution
XIV Alchemy	creativity
XV The Devil	discretion
XVI The Tower	honor
XVII The Star	sincerity, hope
XVIII The Moon	gentleness
XIX The Sun	generosity
XX Aeon	fairness
XXI The Universe	respect
0 The Multiverse	unifying
Blank card (void)	silent

Table X. 11 Yoga Correspondence

Card	Correspondence
0 The Fool	Child
I The Magician	Monkey
II The High Priestess	Cobra
III The Empress	Upward Dog
IV The Emperor	Downward Dog
V Hierophant	Hero
VI The Lovers	Bridge
VII Chariot	Eagle
VIII Strength	Lion
IX The Hermit	Lotus
X The Wheel of Fortune	Wheel
XI Justice	Fish
XII The Hanged Man	Headstand
XIII Death	Corpse
XIV Alchemy	Triangle
XV The Devil	Warrior
XVI The Tower	Thunder Bolt
XVII The Star	Five Pointed Star
XVIII The Moon	Half moon
XIX The Sun	Cat
XX Aeon	Mountain
XXI The Universe	Tree
0 The Multiverse	Crab
Blank card (void)	Table

Bibliography

Banzhaf, Hajo. *Tarot and the Journey of the Hero.*
York Beach, Maine: Samuel Weiser Inc., 2000.

Braden, Nina Lee. *Tarot For Self Discovery.*
St. Paul, Minnesota: Llewellyn, 2002.

Crowley, Aleister. *The Book of Thoth.*
York Beach, Maine: Weiser Books, 2004

Diemer, Deedre. *The ABC's of Chakra Therapy: A Workbook.*
York Beach, Maine: Weiser Books, 1998

DuQuette, Lon Milo. *Tarot of Ceremonial Magick.*
York Beach, Maine: Samuel Weiser, Inc., 1995.

Giles, Cynthia. *The Tarot: Methods, Mystery, and More.*
New York: Fireside Books, 1996.

Lao-Tse. James Legge, translator. *Tao Teh King, or the Tao and Its Characteristics.*
E-text, 1995.

Martin, Joseph Ernest. *The Compass Guide to the Quest Tarot.*
St. Paul, Minnesota: Llewellyn, 2003.

Papus. *The Tarot of the Bohemians.*
North Hollywood, California: Wilshire Book Company, 1971.

Parfitt, Will. *The New Living Qabalah: A Practical and Experiential Guide to Understanding the Tree of Life.* Rockport, MA: Element Books, 1988.

Watts, Alan. *The Way of Zen.*
New York: Random House, 1989.

Web Sites

Abraxas Tarot
http://www.tarot-decks.com

Aeclectic Tarot
http://www.aeclectic.net/tarot/cards

Learning the Tarot
http://www.learntarot.com

Tarot decks
http://www.tarot.com/about-tarot/decks

Yoga Basics
http://www.yogabasics.com/asana

About the Author

Shanddaramon is a published writer, composer, and poet and is the author of several books and articles on living and being a modern Pagan. He lives in the Boston, Massachusetts area with his family where he teaches classes in music. He has often sought ways in which to combine his interest in the arts with a growing interest in the mystical and, specifically, through Paganism. He applies these skills through his art and writing and through services such as divinatory advising, pastoral counseling and ritual work. Combining the arts with mysticism, he has created classes and workshops for others with similar interests and has led rituals for organizations and individuals.

For one year he was a professional Tarot card reader in Vermont but decided that he preferred, instead, to read only for friends and family. He has taught several workshops on reading and applying the Tarot techniques discussed in this book.

Shanddaramon may be contacted by emailing him at mail@shanddaramon.com.

Other Books
by Shanddaramon

For Adults:

1. *Self Initiation for the Solitary Witch: Attaining Higher Spirituality Through a Five Degree System.* New Page Books, 2004.
2. *Living Paganism: An Advanced Guide for the Solitary Practitioner.* New Page Books, 2005.
3. *Dewdrops In The Moonlight: A Book of Pagan Prayer.* Astor Press, 2007.
4. *The Sacred Quest: A Pagan Perspective on the Pursuit of Happiness.* Astor Press, 2008.

For Children:

1. *Sabbats of the Northern Hemisphere: A Pagan Book for Children.* Astor Press, 2008.
2. *The Twelve Days of Yule: A Pagan Children's Activity Book.* Astor Press, 2009.

www.ingramcontent.com/pod-product-compliance
Lightning Source LLC
LaVergne TN
LVHW011417080426
835512LV00005B/105